DATE DUE FOR RETURN		
ON EXHIBITION until 29. NOV. 1989		

GEORGE BERKELEY: ESSAYS AND REPLIES

edited by David Berman

GEORGE BERKELEY

ESSAYS AND REPLIES

edited by David Berman

IRISH ACADEMIC PRESS

in association with

HERMATHENA
TRINITY COLLEGE DUBLIN

This book was printed in the Republic of Ireland
for Irish Academic Press Limited, Kill Lane, Blackrock,
Co Dublin, and for *Hermathena*, Trinity College, Dublin.

It also appears as *Hermathena* CXXXIX (Winter 1985)
edited by J.R. Bartlett, and is
published in book form in 1986.

ISBN 0-7165-2395-7

© *Hermathena* 1985

British Library Cataloguing in Publication Data

George Berkeley: essays and replies
  1. Berkeley, George
  I. Berman, David
    192   B1348

ISBN 0-7165-2395-7

Printed by Cahill Printers Ltd., East Wall Rd., Dublin 3.

Preface

The 300th anniversary of George Berkeley's birth was marked by conferences in Newport, Ottawa, Dublin, Kalamazoo, Cloyne, Compiègne, Oxford and Paris. The papers printed here were originally read at Berkeley's university in Dublin: on Trinity Monday, 6 May 1985, and at a conference, 19-22 August 1985. The conference was attended by scholars from more than fifty universities or colleges, from a dozen countries. I am grateful to Vincent Denard, Tim Williamson, John Gaskin, Michael Slote, Anne Burke and Paul Bagley for help in organizing the conference, and to the Trinity College Dublin Trust for financial assistance.

This volume differs from its 1953 predecessor — *Homage to George Berkeley (1685-1753)* — in two respects. It does not include all the principal papers read at the conference; and it contains not merely principal papers but also replies. Some papers will appear elsewhere; one — by Ernest Sosa — has already been published in *Essays on Berkeley* (Oxford University Press: 1985), and we print only David Armstrong's reply. The themes in our volume range from Berkeley's biography, economics and notebooks, to his connections with Scotland and with Greek scepticism, to central topics in his philosophy: the *esse* is *percipi* principle, abstraction and agency, the active/passive distinction. This collection should indicate something of Berkeley's diversity as well as contemporary scholarly interest in him. For help in selecting and editing the papers I should like to thank John Bartlett, Vincent Denard, David Evans, Ian Tipton, and Tim Williamson. The Index was prepared by Paul Bagley.

DAVID BERMAN

3

Contents

ILLUSTRATIONS

Plate 1: Berkeley, by James Latham, *circa* 1745 (oil on canvas, 29 ins high x 24 ins wide; Senior Common Room, T.C.D.)

Plate 2: Berkeley, by Robert Home, *circa* 1785 (oil on canvas, 109 ins high x 69 ins wide; Examination Hall, T.C.D.)

between pages 24 and 25

(Both portraits are produced by courtesy of the Board of T.C.D.)

Notes on Authors

D. M. Armstrong
B.A. (Sydney), B. PHIL. (Oxon), PH.D. (Melb.), Challis Professor of Philosophy, University of Sydney.

B. Belfrage
PH.D. (Lund), Philosophy Department, University of Lund.

D. Berman
B.A. (N.Y.) M.A. (Dubl., Denver), PH.D., Senior Lecturer in Mental and Moral Science and Fellow of Trinity College, Dublin.

H. M. Bracken
B.A. (Trinity College, Hartford), M.A. (Johns Hopkins), PH.D. (Iowa), Professor of Philosophy, McGill University, Montreal.

G. Brykman
Agrégée de Philosophie, Docteur ès Lettres (Sorbonne), Professeur à l'Université de technologie de Compiègne.

P. H. Kelly
M.A., PH.D (Cantab.), Senior Lecturer in Modern History, Trinity College, Dublin.

R. McKim
B.A. (Dubl.), M.A. (Calgary), PH.D. (Yale), Assistant Professor of Philosophy and Religious Studies, University of Illinois at Urbana-Champaign.

J. P. Murray
B.S. (Marquette), PH.D. (St. Louis U.), Associate Professor of Philosophy, Creighton University, Omaha.

G. S. Pappas
B.A. (Gettysburg College), M.A., PH.D. (University of Pennsylvania), Professor of Philosophy, The Ohio State University.

M. A. Stewart
M.A. (St Andrews), PH.D. (Pennsylvania), Senior Lecturer and Head of Department of Philosophy, University of Lancaster.

A. Stroll
B.A., M.A., PH.D. (University of California, Berkeley), Professor of Philosophy, University of California, San Diego (La Jolla, California).

S. Tweyman
B.A., M.A., PH.D. (Toronto), Professor of Philosophy, Glendon College, York University, Toronto.

K. P. Winkler
B.A. (Trinity College, Connecticut), PH.D. (University of Texas at Austin), Associate Professor of Philosophy at Wellesley College, Massachusetts.

George Berkeley: pictures by Goldsmith, Yeats and Luce

by David Berman

'When the multitude heard, they were astonished at his doctrine'; or so runs the inscription commemorating Berkeley in our College Chapel, an inscription I should like to reformulate: When the biographers heard, they were fascinated by his life; for George Berkeley the man has attracted many biographers. These include at least one major poet, a British Prime Minister, a psychoanalyst and a famous novelist. And yet, amidst the diversity, the work of three biographers — Joseph Stock, A.C. Fraser and the late A.A. Luce — stands out.

Joseph Stock was the pioneer; a Fellow of this College, his *Account of the life of . . . Berkeley* was first published in 1776 and often reissued over the next forty years. As Stock was Berkeley's foremost biographer in the eighteenth century, so Fraser, a Scotsman, established himself as the leading Berkeley scholar of the nineteenth century by his massive 1871 *Life and letters of Berkeley*. Fraser set a precedent not only for high scholarship but also for longevity — in both of which he was followed by *his* great successor, Dr Luce, who, like Fraser, lived into his nineties, and, like Stock, was a distinguished Fellow of this College.

Luce's biographical pre-eminence rests firmly on his *Life of Berkeley*, universally accepted as authoritative since its appearance in 1949. Drawing skilfully on the primary evidence — much of which he himself brought to light — Luce there reveals Berkeley as a man of strong sense, 'sane, shrewd, efficient',[1] a picture that complements his commonsense reading of Berkeley's philosophy. Among the factors that helped the biography to achieve its magisterial position — a position never attained by the philosophical reading — is one I want to stress here, namely Luce's deep appreciation of his predecessors. About Stock and Fraser he comments:

> Stock had access to family information, and he laid the foundations upon which later biographers have built, but his [*Account*] was too slender and brief. Fraser had more success. His *Life and letters* is a mine for biographers . . .; but [its] portrait of Berkeley lacks depth and tone, and in some features is untrue.[2]

9

David Berman

Even more untrue, according to Luce, was the first biographical essay on Berkeley, printed in the *British Plutarch* in 1762. Luce scathingly describes it as a

> pretentious, and irresponsible account . . . the source of the general misconception of the man, the *fons et origo mali* . . . The Memoir contains at least three definite errors in fact which can be easily refuted. . . . Its picture of Berkeley in his student days is absurd; he is a recluse and the butt of college, and is by some regarded as 'the greatest dunce in the whole university'; here we have the well-known but baseless, tale, told with gusto, of him and his [student] chum, Contarini, agreeing to hang one another for a while in turn that they might experience the sensations of dying. . . The Memoir contains a few interesting and possibly true statements which are not found elsewhere; but . . . it looks like a piece of ignorant hack-work without a vestige of authority. . . . That a bantering record of this great man . . . [concludes Luce] should have been the first to appear and should have set the tone for later studies is a matter for keen regret.[3]

Dr Luce's own portrait of Berkeley as 'the man of affairs, sane, shrewd, efficient' is in clear opposition to this early memoir. But Luce was also reacting to another, more recent misrepresentation, as he saw it, namely, the picture of Berkeley which emerges in the work of W.B. Yeats, particularly in the poet's *Diary* of 1930 and in his fifteen-page Introduction to Hone and Rossi's *Bishop Berkeley*, published in the following year. For Yeats the real Berkeley was 'that fierce young man', a visionary and radical who 'proved all things a dream'.[4] Indeed, according to Yeats, there were two Berkeleys. Berkeley was 'idealist and realist alike'. He 'wore an alien mask'. Only in his student notebooks, the *Philosophical commentaries*, 'is Berkeley sincere . . . the bishop was a humbug'.[5] Dr Luce's comment, in a word, is *nonsense*: Yeats's assertions, he says, are 'charming inconsequent nonsense, sparkles of poetic fancy without any foundation in fact. There was only one George Berkeley in actual life; he never wore a mask, and he was transparently honest and single-minded.'[6] Dr Luce told me that he sent Yeats a detailed critique, to which the poet did not, however, reply.

Curiously, each man focussed his biographical *animus* on a particular Berkeley portrait, both of which are hanging here in Trinity. Thus Yeats exclaimed: 'I hate what I remember of his portrait [figure 1] in the Fellows Room [that is, Senior Common Room] at Trinity College; it wears a mask kept by . . . painters . . . of the eighteenth century for certain admired men.'[7] 'That philanthropic

10

Pictures by Goldsmith, Yeats and Luce

serene Bishop, that pasteboard man never wrote the [*Philosophical commentaries.*][8] (One wonders what Yeats would have said had he learned that this hated portrait, by James Latham, has appeared on an Irish postage stamp commemorating the philosopher.[9]) The portrait Dr Luce disliked he explicitly associated with Yeats. 'The false Berkeley Yeats knew is the Berkeley of legend [wrote Luce] . . . it is the long-haired, languishing visionary depicted in that mural decoration [figure 2] which does duty as portrait of Berkeley in the Examination Hall of his College . . .'[10] It is 'the stage philosopher peering into infinity'.[11]

Of course, Luce's own biographical portrait of Berkeley was formed by many forces, positive as well as negative; among the positive ones are the statements of Berkeley's wife and daughter-in-law, the researches of Benjamin Rand; more negatively, the work of Hone and Rossi and also John Wild. But the main negative influence was what we may call the Goldsmith/Yeats picture. I call it that because, unknown to Luce (and Yeats), we now know that Oliver Goldsmith was the author of that first notorious memoir, 'the *fons et origo mali*'.[12]

What I should like to do, then, is to consider the implications of this surprising development; for the discovery of Goldsmith's authorship by his recent editor, Arthur Friedman, has, I hope to show, a direct bearing on the credibility of that earliest memoir and, of course, on our understanding of Berkeley. I shall then consider some additional evidence — much of it new — which bears on the biographical controversy between Luce and Yeats. Before doing so, however, it will be useful if I pause to sketch the clear, uncontroversial outline of Berkeley's life and work.

George Berkeley, Ireland's most famous philosopher, was born 300 years ago, on 12 March 1685. His early years were spent at Dysart Castle, 2 miles from Thomastown, in Co. Kilkenny. After four years at Kilkenny College, Berkeley entered Trinity College in 1700, where he was elected a scholar in 1702 and a Fellow in 1707. In 1709, at the age of 24, he published his *Essay towards a new theory of vision* — a landmark in the history of psychology — which Adam Smith later described as 'one of the finest examples of philosophical analysis . . . to be found . . . in any . . . language'.[13] In 1710, the year he was ordained, Berkeley issued his most celebrated work, *The principles of human knowledge*, which expounds his immaterialistic philosophy. The *Principles* were not, however, well received. Attributing this partly to style and presentation, Berkeley recast his philosophy in the *Three dialogues between Hylas and Philonous*, printed in 1713, a work still studied as pure literature. It is upon these three books, each a masterpiece, that Berkeley's reputation as a cultural leader chiefly rests. They entitle him to be ranked with Plato, Spinoza and Kant. It is gratifying to record here, therefore, that on the title-pages of all three books the author is identified as 'George Berkeley, M.A. Fellow of Trinity College, Dublin'. Even more than Swift, Goldsmith or Burke — those other Trinity demi-gods — Berkeley is, in the fullest sense, a son of this College. For not only was he a Trinity graduate, scholar, Fellow and teacher, but his world-fame derives from the philosophical work he accomplished here, in those heroic years between 1707 and 1713.

Although my theme is Berkeley's life, rather than his doctrine, I cannot omit saying something of the philosophy. Its main thesis is that matter does not exist; hence the name *immaterialism*. To many this has seemed outrageous, as our Chapel inscription bears witness. Yet what is matter? If it is what we see and touch, then Berkeley does not deny it. But what do we see and touch, one may ask, if not material things? Berkeley's answer is that we perceive only sensible qualities or ideas: 'By sight [he states in the *Principles*] I have the ideas of light and colours . . . By touch I perceive . . . hard and soft, heat and cold, motion and resistance . . . . Smelling furnishes me with odours; the palate with tastes, and hearing conveys sounds to the mind.'[14] So I know there is a sheet of paper before me because I see a whitish patch, feel the smooth rectangular shape, and smell the distinctive papery fragrance. The paper's existence consists in being perceived.

Why, then, bring in matter? Indeed, what is the matter of the paper? For some, it is the inert substance which supports and causes the paper's sensible qualities. Yet how, asks Berkeley, can we know this material substance if we cannot perceive it? And how can it support and cause sensible qualities, like odours, if it is nonsentient and inert? To say that the material paper is imperceptible but resembles our perception of it, is, Berkeley argues, as nonsensical as saying that an odour is like something that cannot be smelled.

Now to suggest — as I have — that immaterialism is formidable is not to imply that Berkeley exploded all conceptions of matter, or that his philosophy consists solely in such explosions. For Berkeley only two kinds of things exist: minds and ideas. (Few philosophies are so economical.) The Infinite Mind, God, produces sensible ideas in finite minds, such as ourselves. We, too, are able to produce weaker versions of these ideas in memory and imagination, and by so doing we gain some notion of God's orderly creation of our world of sensible ideas. In short, God replaces matter: He causes, supports, and guarantees the reality of the world of sense.

Berkeley's immaterialism is easier to dismiss than to refute. Probably no philosopher has been dispatched and resurrected as often as Berkeley. As one poet wrote in 1745: 'Coxcombs vanquish Berkeley by a grin.'[15] Not long after, Dr Johnson vainly tried to refute Berkeley's immaterialism by kicking a stone — without realizing that the resistance and hardness he felt are entirely real for Berkeley, because entirely perceptible.[16] In this century, Lenin interrupted his revolutionary activities to attack Berkeley's immaterialism and its modern (covert) followers. Following Lenin's lead, Berkeley continues to be esteemed in the Soviet Union as an *honest* subjective idealist.[17] In Europe he is considered the father of modern idealism. In America he is honoured as a precursor of pragmatism.[18] Wherever philosophy is taught, there, almost certainly, one will find the three books Berkeley wrote here at Trinity.

Although his connection with College lasted officially until 1724, when he was appointed Dean of Derry, most of his time from 1713 to 1724 was spent away from Ireland and philosophy. In England he wrote for the *Guardian* (1713) and became friendly with Swift, Pope, Steele and Addison. In France and Italy he travelled extensively, crossing the Alps in mid-winter, observing at close quarters an eruption of Mount Vesuvius. By 1722, however, he had turned his attention from the Old to the New World, and boldly determined to found a college in Bermuda. The college, as he explained in his *Proposal* of 1724, was to educate the American colonists and train Indian missionaries to the Indians. During the next decade Berkeley's charm, courage and practicality were amply demonstrated by the wide backing he gained for his project. He received large private subscriptions; obtained a Royal charter and was promised £20,000 by the British government. Even more surprising, Swift's Vanessa left him nearly half her fortune, a legacy Berkeley described as 'providential'.[19] In 1729, newly married, he set sail for Rhode Island, which was to be a base for his projected college. Here he lived for nearly three years, waiting in vain for the promised grant. In late 1731 he returned to London, having been told that the money would never be paid.

Berkeley's second main period of authorship now begins in 1732 with *Alciphron . . . an apology for the Christian religion* — composed in

Rhode Island — followed by the *Theory of vision vindicated* (1733) and *The analyst* (1734) — a book which one historian has called 'the most spectacular mathematical event in the eighteenth-century in England'.[20] After two years in London, Berkeley was appointed to the bishopric of Cloyne, where he spent the next seventeen years. In 1735-7 he published his *Querist*, composed of nearly 1,000 questions on Irish economic and social matters. From the goods of mind and fortune, Berkeley turned lastly to the good of the body. In *Siris: a chain of philosophical reflexions* (1744), his most enigmatic work, he championed the drinking of tar-water, a medicine of which he learned from America and to which he ascribed universal curative powers. Within a month after publication, *Siris* and tar-water had become the rage. Much of the Bishop's time was now devoted to defending his medicine and ministering to patients. In late 1752 he left Cloyne, to supervise his son's education in Oxford. There on 14 January 1753 died that 'excellently great and very good man' — as Berkeley was then described.[21] He was buried in the chapel of Christ Church, Oxford.

Here, then, is the bare outline of Berkeley's life and works. Nor would it have been difficult to fill in the sketch with other well-documented details displaying the familiar Berkeley — with every virtue under heaven. Yet, particularly here and now — at the University of Stock and Luce, in the tercentenary of Berkeley's birth — I felt that such a familiar display would hardly be fitting. So instead, I should like to return to the controversial question raised earlier, that is, how much truth is there in the Goldsmith/Yeats picture of Berkeley, the picture so roundly repudiated by Dr Luce? Now, as I mentioned, Dr Luce did not know that Goldsmith was the author of the first memoir. Nor should anyone, I imagine, if a unique copy of the first printing had not been noticed by Prof. Friedman in the Huntington Library at San Marino, California. For the 1762 memoir, as we now know, was originally printed in 1759/60 in the *Weekly Magazine*, a short-lived periodical in which Goldsmith published some of his earliest verse.

More decisive still, there is a crucial phrase in this first printing of the memoir that was omitted from the later reprints known to Luce, Yeats and others. It occurs in the long, circumstantial hanging anecdote. Here we learn that, after Berkeley had been 'tied up to the ceiling, and the chair taken from under his feet, his [student] companion', Contarine, waited so long to assist Berkeley that 'as

Pictures by Goldsmith, Yeats and Luce

soon as Berkeley was taken down he fell senseless and motionless upon the floor. After some trouble however [he] was brought to himself; and observing his band [exclaimed] bless my heart, Contarine, you have quite rumpled my band.'[22] Now in the *Weekly Magazine* the writer not only names Berkeley's companion but says that it was Contarine 'from whom I had the story' (*ibid*). Who, then, was this Contarine? There has been only one Contarine at Trinity College and that was the Reverend Thomas Contarine who entered College in 1701 — a year after Berkeley — and graduated in 1706. Equally important, this Thomas Contarine was the uncle and patron of Goldsmith; indeed, he helped to pay Oliver's expenses at Trinity. Goldsmith refers to his uncle in the *Deserted village* in the line: 'More skilled to raise the wretched than to rise'.[23] (Would I be stretching it, if I suggest that Goldsmith is alluding here not only to his uncle's generosity but also to his skill in hanging poor Berkeley up to the ceiling, but evading the proposal — as the memoir puts it — when it was his 'turn to go up'?)

On the memoir's authorship, Prof. Friedman notes: 'Of the small number of men who would be employed in writing for the *Weekly Magazine*, it is highly improbable that anyone except Goldsmith himself would have known his uncle, who spent his [entire] life in Ireland.'[24] But why, one might ask, was the crucial phrase 'from whom I had the story' omitted from the *British Plutarch* reprint? The answer, I believe, is that because its biographies were presented in the first person plural, it would have been absurd for the *Plutarch's* piratical editors to have written 'and from whom *we* had the story'.

Once we allow — as I think we must — Goldsmith's authorship of the memoir, we can no longer regard the memoir as, to quote Luce's judgment, 'a piece of ignorant hack-work without a vestige of authority.' For not only could Goldsmith have drawn on his generous uncle Contarine — at whose house he often stayed after leaving College — but he could also have gleaned biographical information from another well-placed relative, the Reverend Isaac Goldsmith, who was Dean of Cloyne from 1736 to 1769, in other words, for fifteen years during which Berkeley was Bishop. The memoir's credibility has also been bolstered recently from another source. One of its (apparently) dubious statements has been corroborated, I think, by the independent testimony of Berkeley's wife. In the memoir, Goldsmith had asserted that 'Doctor Pepusch, an excellent Musician [was] engaged in [Berkeley's] design to establish a College in Bermuda, and actually embarked in order to put it into execution, but the ship being cast away the design unhappily was discontinued . . .'[25] Because the latter part of this statement was known to be untrue, the first part has also been rejected. Yet in her annotated copy of Stock's *Account of Berkeley*, recently acquired by our College Library, Mrs Berkeley notes that 'one of the first composers and performers in Music of that time had engaged to come' to Bermuda — a reference, I take it, to John Christopher Pepusch, who arranged the music for Gay's *The Beggar's Opera*.[26]

My conclusion is that Goldsmith's picture of Berkeley cannot now be confidently dismissed. Moreover, his picture fits, in some measure, with that of Yeats; for the youthful visionary, who proved all things a dream, might indeed appear absurd and comical to his fellow students — he might well seem, as Goldsmith puts it, 'the greatest genius or the greatest dunce in the whole university . . .', 'a fool' to those 'slightly acquainted with him', a 'prodigy of learning and good nature to those who shared his intimate friendship'. And while we may not have here the two Berkeleys, as claimed by Yeats, we at least have two very different views of him. The Goldsmith and Yeats accounts cohere also in another interesting respect. It is the young, Trinity-College Berkeley whom Goldsmith and Yeats both see as solitary and especially childlike. The later Berkeley becomes in Goldsmith's memoir more sober; whereas for Yeats, he became more circumspect about revealing his true self. In later years, Yeats claimed, Berkeley's deeper, more anarchic self appears 'but in glimpses or as something divined or inferred'. Perhaps the agreement and coherence of the Goldsmith/Yeats pictures come out most clearly when juxtaposed to Luce's portrait of the straightforward Berkeley, 'sane, efficient, shrewd', the man with vision but in no sense a visionary.

Who, then, saw the real Berkeley? Perhaps I should note at this point that our knowledge of Berkeley is probably very limited. Like other prominent eighteenth-century figures, he seems to have kept himself to himself — which has led some to regard the eighteenth century as an era of superficiality. Certainly, Berkeley was not given to self-revelation, particularly about his early life. Thus, we know virtually nothing of his parents, and the only personal detail we learn of his childhood is from his cryptic note-book entry 'Mem. that I was distrustful at 8 years old . . .'[27] Nor have we many more details of his student life, for our main source for that period is Goldsmith's memoir, such as it is. Berkeley wrote no account of his life; and very few of his letters, comparatively speaking, have come down to us. We have neither letter nor even note between himself and any member of his family. Dr Luce published 270 of his letters

16

Pictures by Goldsmith, Yeats and Luce

in 1956; since then about 20 new letters have been discovered. But compare that to the published correspondence of Berkeley's two colleagues in the triumvirate of British Empiricism — 1,500 letters for Locke, 600 letters for Hume — and one sees how small the extant Berkeley correspondence is. Yet it is from this source that Luce's portrait is mainly drawn. For Yeats, on the other hand, the real Berkeley, the angry rebel behind an 'alien mask', is to be seen in Berkeley's student notebooks. Only once, Yeats wrote, was Berkeley 'free, when, still an undergraduate [and young Fellow] he filled . . . [his notebooks] . . . with snorts of defiance'.[28] Yeats delighted particularly in those four snorts where Berkeley wrote 'We Irishmen', for 'That [Yeats declared] was the birth of the [Irish] national intellect; and it aroused the defeat in Berkeley's philosophical secret society of English materialism, the Irish Salamis.'[29] Luce, however, disputed this, arguing that when Berkeley wrote 'We Irishmen,' he simply meant 'we ordinary folk, shrewd judges of fact and commonsense'.[30] Luce also argued against Yeats's other fond belief that Berkeley belonged to a secret society devoted to immaterialism. Both issues are a little complicated, but I think it is clear that Luce was right: Yeats was carried away by wishful thinking.

Plainly, a follower of Yeats will not find it easy — even given the new Goldsmith identification — to dislodge Luce's sturdy portrait. For not only is it drawn skilfully from the available primary evidence, but it is broadly supported by earlier biographers, notably by Stock and (with qualification) by Fraser; more recently, by Lord Balfour and Benjamin Rand. Neither Goldsmith nor Yeats could lay claim to their wide acquaintance with Berkeley's life and writings. Luce's picture of the straightforward, sane Berkeley has been confirmed also in a detailed book — published five years ago — on the psychology of philosophers. There Berkeley appears as one of the most normal philosophers of the past 300 years.[31] And yet, perhaps the poets did see something that the scholars missed.

Clearly the question is complicated. For one thing, some of Goldsmith's statements tend to support Luce's disagreement with Fraser on the Cloyne period. Whereas Fraser portrayed Berkeley as 'the recluse of Cloyne' — 'a caricature', according to Luce[32] — Goldsmith paints a picture more gregarious and more in line with that of Luce: 'The gentlemen of the neighbourhood and he [says Goldsmith in his memoir] preserved the closest intimacy; and while [the Bishop] cultivated the duties of his station, he was not unmindful of the innocent amusements of life: music he was

17

particularly fond of, and always kept one or two exquisite performers to amuse his hours of leisure.'[33] About one such performer, the Italian musician Pasquilino, we have a story from Berkeley's daughter-in-law which adds colour to Goldsmith's picture and weight to Luce's case against Fraser. One day at dinner, we are told, the Bishop mentioned that he had disposed of a great many concert tickets for Pasquilino among his neighbours, to which the Italian replied with a bow: 'May God *pickle* your Lordship.' After the laughter of the company subsided, the poor Italian said, 'Vell, in de grammar dat my Lord gave me . . . it is printed, *pickle,* to keep from decay.'[34]

My serious point in all this is to emphasize that we are not being asked to choose between two clearcut, rival pictures of Berkeley. It is not as though Luce, Fraser and Stock saw one Berkeley, Goldsmith and Yeats another. A further difficulty is that given Yeats's impressionistic sketch — in some ways almost a prose poem — it is not altogether clear how completely it differs from that of Luce. I take it, however, that the hanging episode, recorded by Goldsmith, and the young Berkeley's description of himself in entry 465 of his notebooks, agree with Yeats's picture. Here Berkeley writes: 'I am young, I am an upstart, I am a pretender, I am vain, very well. I shall Endeavour patiently to bear up under the most lessening, villifying appellations that the pride & rage of man can devise.'[35] The image this 'snort of defiance' — to use Yeats's phrase — conjures up *is* of a rebellious young man, and it is supported by some new evidence, the testimony of Archbishop King, another distinguished graduate. It has long been known that because Berkeley was ordained without the Archbishop's permission, he was forced to apologize to King, which he did in a letter of 18 April 1710. Dr Luce's comment is: 'The incident did not reflect in any way on Berkeley, who was a victim of a trial of strength between the university and the Archbishop [who] was not an enemy . . . of Berkeley' (*Life,* pp. 43-4). However, a letter I found from King to Ashe, the Bishop who ordained Berkeley, argues otherwise. For there King wryly observes:

> . . . your Ldp alledges that Mr Berkly was in a great haste [to be ordained.] I believe he was as soon as my back was turned, but tho' it be three years . . . since he was fellow, yet he never aplyd to me nor I suppose wou'd if I had bin in Dublin, and yet phaps it had not bin the worse for him, if I had discoursed him as I do others before ordination . . .'[36]

Pictures by Goldsmith, Yeats and Luce

From this it seems that King — who, it is generally agreed, was a shrewd judge of character — saw the young junior fellow as a vain upstart, rebellious and arrogant. But this is still a long way from the subterranean Berkeley, whom Yeats describes as 'solitary, talkative, ecstatic, destructive'.[37]

However, consider the following dictum of Berkeley recorded by his wife, Anne: The Bishop's 'maxim', she says,

> was that nothing very good or very bad could be done until a man entirely got the better of fear of *que dira-t-on* — but when a man has overcome himself he overcomes the world and then is fitted for his *Master's use* —[38]

I find this maxim revealing, particularly when taken with another, this time recorded by Berkeley's friend, Lord Percival: ' "I know not what it is to fear", said Mr Berkeley, "but I have a delicate sense of danger".'[39] Both dicta seem to reveal a duality. In the first, there is what people say, public opinion, the world or the worldly; this one must cease to fear if one is to do something either very good or very bad. The other dictum suggests that Berkeley had a natural lack of fear — but of what? I am tempted to combine the two dicta and say that he was naturally fearless of *que dira-t-on*, of what the world says, and that this helps to explain those three bold crusades which largely constitute his life and career — his attempt to reform philosophy in early life by proving the non-existence of matter; his scheme in middle age to establish an arts and missionary college, to ameliorate British society in the New World; and, finally, his advocacy of tar-water as a universal medicine.

Any one of these three projects might have marked its originator as a Don Quixote. Yet that caricature simply does not fit Berkeley. For in each of his three idealistic projects we clearly see the practical man and cautious reasoner, the man with his feet set firmly on the ground, who anticipates and answers our best objections. Berkeley was no romantic, like his immaterialist follower Shelley, carried away by a noble idea in the blaze of its inception. Each of Berkeley's three projects he publicised only after he had privately deliberated for at least two years. So, while Berkeley may naturally have lacked fear of public opinion, he knew what was needed to persuade others, to alter public opinion. Naturally unworldly, perhaps, he had a delicate sense of what was required if the world was to be changed. In the non-philosophical sense, at least, Berkeley was both an

19

idealist and a realist. There is nothing languid, dreaming or visionary in the way that he campaigns for his immaterialism, his Bermuda College or his universal medicine. And yet the goals were extraordinary — astonishing — as Berkeley himself recognised. That he should seriously entertain and publicly defend them — *that* strikes me as visionary and child-like. Yet once we encounter him actually defending them, then we feel that he is the very paradigm of reason. David Hume seems to have felt something of this when he said of Berkeley's philosophical arguments: '*They admit of no answer, and* [yet] *produce no conviction.* '[40] One does have the impression, as Yeats suggests, that Berkeley lived in two worlds. We feel at one moment that his ideas are *out of this world,* at another moment we cannot see what *in the world* is wrong with them.

Berkeley's friends, too, seem to have perceived and been struck by the way he combined innocence and experience, shrewdness and selflessness. Thus in 1713 Richard Steele wrote to him: 'Till I knew you, I thought it the privilege of angels only to be very knowing and very innocent'[41] — a tribute supported by Bishop Atterbury, who said of Berkeley:

> So much understanding, so much knowledge, so much innocence, and such humility, I did not think had been the portion of any but angels till I saw this gentleman.[42]

Pope's better-known line — 'To *Berkley,* ev'ry Virtue under Heav'n'[43] — dulls rather than sharpens what I take to be the crucial insight: that Berkeley united the (seemingly) incompatible virtues of worldly wisdom and childlike innocence. Certainly Swift saw Berkeley's innocent and unworldly side when in 1724 he described him as 'an absolute philosopher with regard to money, titles, and power'.[44] Yet Thomas Blackwell, Berkeley's Scottish friend, was plainly impressed by his other side when he wrote:

> I scarce remember to have conversed with [Mr. Berkeley] on [any] art, liberal or mechanic, of which he knew not more than the ordinary practitioners . . . . With the widest views, he descended into . . . minute detail . . . . I have known him sit for hours in forgeries and founderies to inspect their successive operations.[45]

Perhaps Berkeley's capacity to unite other-worldly idealism with this-worldly practicality helps to explain the extraordinary impression he made on the London wits. Thus, there is a story told by Lord Bathurst about a meeting of the Scriblerus Club at his house,

Pictures by Goldsmith, Yeats and Luce

where all the members rallied Berkeley on his Bermuda scheme: ' . . . having listened to all the lively things they had to say, [we are told that Berkeley] begged to be heard in his turn; and displayed his plan with such an astonishing and animating force of eloquence and enthusiasm, that they were struck dumb, and, after some pause, rose up all together with earnestness, exclaiming — "Let us all set out with him immediately [for Bermuda]".'[46]

I am *tempted*, then, to agree with Yeats that there *was* a deep, unworldly, childlike side to Berkeley. But Yeats was wrong to suppose that Berkeley the Bishop was a humbug. For the deep Berkeley was inextricably bound with the religious man, the Christian, whose aim, as Mrs Berkeley says, was to be 'fitted for his *Master's use*'. That comes out clearly in all three of Berkeley's bold crusades — they are all deeply motivated or guided by his religion. Indeed, it is in Berkeley's zealous commitment to Christianity that we glimpse him, in my opinion, at his unworldly worst: in his Biblical endorsement of slavery; in his approval of kidnapping (for the sake of converting the American indians); in his theological rejection of all rebellion — even if a tyrant were guilty of the most heinous acts; in his suggestion that irreligion should be considered a capital crime no less serious than treason.[47]

Where can the real Berkeley be found? Well, one answer is to go first to our Common Room portrait (which Yeats disliked) and then to the painting in the Examination Hall (which Luce disliked). Clearly, however, that would be facile. The painting in the Examination Hall is an imaginative recreation, with no real authority; whereas there is every reason to believe that Bishop Berkeley did sit for the Latham portrait. Similarly, there can be little doubt that Berkeley sat for Luce's biographical portrait, given its judicious use of Berkeley's correspondence and other hard evidence. Neither Goldsmith nor Yeats inspires such confidence. Goldsmith was well-known for mixing truth and fantasy. Similarly, most of Yeats's judgments are based not on evidence but on intuition, as when he asserts that with Berkeley 'we feel perhaps for the first time that eternity is always at our heels or hidden from our eyes by the thickness of a door',[48] an assertion which must prompt the question: Is this biography or poetry? And yet for all that, a suspicion remains — as I have tried to show — that there *is* a deeper, wilder and more uncanny Berkeley which neither Latham nor Luce has captured, but of whom Goldsmith and Yeats have caught a distant glimpse.[49]

David Berman

Notes

1. *The Life of George Berkeley, Bishop of Cloyne* (London, 1949), p. 1; referred to hereafter as *Life*.
2. *Life*, Preface, p. v.
3. *Life*, p. 2.
4. J.M. Hone and M.M. Rossi, *Bishop Berkeley: his life, writings, and philosophy* (London, 1931); 'Berkeley: an introduction', by Yeats, p. xv; *The variorum edition of the poems of W.B. Yeats* (London, 1957), 'Blood and the moon', p. 481.
5. W.B. Yeats, *Pages from a diary written in nineteen hundred and thirty* (Dublin, 1944), pp. 38 and 41; *Bishop Berkeley*, Introduction, pp. xxiii and xxvi. Most of this is quoted by Luce in his *Berkeley's immaterialism* (London, 1945), Preface, p. viii.
6. Luce, *Berkeley's immaterialism*, p. viii.
7. *Bishop Berkeley*, Introduction, p. xvi.
8. *Pages from a diary*, p. 38. For a helpful account of Yeats's connection with Berkeley, see D.T. Torchiana, *W. B. Yeats and Georgian Ireland* (Evanston, 1966), pp. 222-265.
9. This 44p stamp, designed by Brendan Donegan, was issued by *An Post* on Thursday, 20 June 1985.
10. *Berkeley's immaterialism*, pp. viii-ix.
11. *Life*, p. 248.
12. Arthur Friedman, *Collected works of Oliver Goldsmith* (Oxford, 1966), vol. 3, p. 35.
13. Adam Smith, *Essays on philosophical subjects* (Dublin, 1795), p. 294.
14. *Works of George Berkeley* (London, 1948-1957), edited by A.A. Luce and T. E. Jessop, vol. 2, p. 41 (referred to as *Works*).
15. John Brown, *Essay on satire, occasioned by the death of Mr. Pope* (1745); in *A collection of poems in six volumes* (London, 1770), vol. 3, p. 328.
16. J. Boswell, *Life of Samuel Johnson* (London, 1831), edited by J.W. Croker, vol. 1, p. 484.
17. In his main philosophical work, *Materialism and empirio-criticism* (1909), Lenin writes: 'Frankly and bluntly did Bishop Berkeley argue! In our own time these very same thoughts . . . are enveloped in a much more artful form . . .', and ' . . . the "recent" Machists have not adduced a single argument against the materialists that had not been adduced by Bishop Berkeley'". (Lenin, *Collected works* (Moscow, 1972), vol. 14, pp. 28 and 38. Also see H.R. Cathcart, "Berkeley's philosophy through Soviet eyes", *Hermathena* 98 (1964), pp. 33-42.
18. R.H. Popkin, 'Berkeley's influence on American philosophy', *Hermathena* 82 (1953), pp. 136-8.
19. Letter to Percival, 4 June 1723, in *Works*, vol. 8, p. 130.
20. F. Cajori, *History of mathematics* (2nd. edition, New York, 1919), p. 236.
21. See Fraser, *Life and letters*, p. 352. The description is by Thomas Secker, later Archbishop of Canterbury.
22. 'Some original memoirs of the late famous Bishop of Cloyne', reprinted in Friedman, *Collected works of Oliver Goldsmith* (see note 12), vol. 3, p. 35.
23. This identification was first made in Charles O'Conor's *The memoirs of the life and writings of the late Charles O'Conor of Balangare* (Dublin, circa 1796), p. 186.
24. Friedman, *Collected works*, vol. 3, p. 37.
25. *Collected works*, vol. 3, p. 35.
26. See my 'Mrs Berkeley's annotations in her interleaved copy of *An account of the life of George Berkeley* (1776), *Hermathena* 122 (1977), pp. 20 and 26. Another piece of new evidence, which seems to lend support to the memoir, is to be found in the hitherto unnoticed 'Last Will . . . of Mrs. Elizabeth Berkeley . . . [daughter-in-law] . . . of the Celebrated Bishop of Cloyne.' This extraordinary document, now in our College Library (ms. no. 3530), is composed of more than 130 folios. In the main part of the Will, dated 1793, Eliza speaks of ' . . . the poor insane Son and Daughter of Bishop Berkeley' (f. 20), who are elsewhere identified as 'Henry Berkeley Esq, eldest son of Bp Berkeley and his sister Mrs Julia Berkeley . . . poor suffering persons in their melancholy situations . . . ' (f. 8). Berkeley was survived

by three children: Henry, Julia and George (the husband of Eliza). Little or nothing has come down to us of Henry and Julia — certainly nothing of their insanity. Yet there may well be a hint of it in the memoir, where Goldsmith mentions that Berkeley drank tar-water 'in abundance himself, and attempted to mend the constitution of his children by the same regimen: this, however, he could never effect, and perhaps his desire of improving their health *and their understanding*, at which he laboured most assiduously, might have *impaired* both' (*Collected works*, p. 40; my italics).

27. *Berkeley, Philosophical commentaries* (Ohio, 1976), edited by G.H. Thomas, with explanatory notes by A.A. Luce; entry 266, p.31.

28. *Pages from a diary*, p.41.

29. *Ibid*, p. 51.

30. See *Philosophical commentaries* (1976), p. 226, and Torchiana (see note 8) pp. 237-8.

31. Ben-Ami Scharfstein, *The philosophers: their lives and the nature of their thought* (Oxford, 1980), p. 182.

32. *Life*, p. 186.

33. *Collected works*, p. 40.

34. *Poems by the late George Monck Berkeley* (London, 1797), Preface (by Eliza Berkeley), p. ccccxii.

35. *Philosophical commentaries* (entry 465), pp. 58-9.

36. Trinity College, Library MS 750/11; see my 'Berkeley and King', *Notes and Queries* New Series 29, no. 6 (1982), pp. 529-30.

37 *Bishop Berkeley*, Introduction, p. xvi.

38. 'Mrs Berkeley's annotations . . . ' (see note 26), p. 22.

39. First published by Luce in 'More unpublished Berkeley letters and new Berkeleiana', *Hermathena* 48 (1933), p. 28.

40. Hume, *Essays and treatises* (Edinburgh, 1793), vol. II, p. 610.

41. *Works*, vol. 7, pp. 176-7.

42. *Letters by several eminent persons deceased including . . . John Hughs . . .* (London, 1772), vol. 2, p. 2.

43. Pope, 'Epilogue to the *Satires*', Dialogue II, in *Pope : Poetical works* (London, 1966), edited by H. Davis, p.417.

44. Swift, letter of 3 Sept. 1724 to Carteret. In a letter to the Earl of Oxford, 14 Aug. 1725, Swift describes Berkeley as 'a true philosopher . . . but of a very visionary virtue . . . ' (*The Correspondence of Jonathan Swift* (London, 1910-14) ed. F.E. Ball, vol. 3, pp. 212-13, 262.

45. Blackwell, *Memoirs of the court of Augustus* (Edinburgh, 1755), vol. 2, pp. 277-8.

46. Quoted in Fraser, *Life and letters*, p.106.

47. See *Proposal*, in *Works*, vol. 7, pp. 346-7 and my 'Berkeley, Christianity and slavery', *The Freethinker* 101 (1981), pp. 52-3; *Passive obedience* (1712), in *Works*, vol. 6, pp. 18, 43-4; and *An essay towards preventing the ruin of Great Britain*, in *Works*, vol. 6, pp. 70-1.

48. *Bishop Berkeley*, Introduction, pp. xxi-ii.

49. This paper was originally delivered as the 1985 Trinity Monday Discourse.

GEORGE BERKELEY D.D.
Fellow 1707, *Bishop of Cloyne* 1733

Plate 1: Berkeley by James Latham, *circa* 1745 (oil on canvas, 29 ins high × 24 ins wide; Senior Common Room, T.C.D.)

Plate 2: Berkeley by Robert Home, *circa* 1785 (Oil on canvas, 109 ins high × 69 ins wide; Examination Hall, T.C.D.)

Berkeley and the Rankenian Club

by M.A. Stewart

Berkeley's philosophy — or what was perceived to be Berkeley's philosophy — was a strong influence upon the intellectual currents in 18th-century Scotland. This much has been a matter of common knowledge, or at least common belief, ever since that period. But the nature of the influence has been distorted and obscured in the mythology that has come to surround the story of a Locke-Berkeley-Hume tradition in the history of philosophy. Some recent scholars have gone back to the 18th-century origins of that story in tracing the Berkeley connection to the Rankenian Club at Edinburgh.[1] In this paper I set out fairly summarily what is to be found if one tries to get behind the legends and piece together the hard evidence; fuller analysis of the materials must wait for another occasion.

The first recorded reference to a link between Berkeley and the Rankenian Club seems to be one occurring half a century after the supposed event, in an anonymous obituary for the Rev. Robert Wallace in the *Scots Magazine* for July 1771. The obituarist traced the foundation of the club to 1717 and identified Wallace as a charter member.[2]

> Among others the abstruse principles vented by Dr. Berkeley, Bishop of Cloyne, were accurately canvassed in it; and the society amused themselves by maintaining with that eminent and pious prelate (to whom Mr Pope, in his *One thousand seven hundred and thirty-eight*, ascribes *every virtue under heaven*) a literary correspondence, in which they pushed his singular tenets all the amazing length to which they have been carried in later publications. To their letters his Lordship transmitted polite and regular returns, endeavouring to avoid the consequences drawn from his doctrines: He was greatly pleased, too, with the extraordinary acuteness and peculiar ingenuity displayed in them, and he has been heard to say, that no persons understood his system better than this set of young gentlemen in North Britain. Hence he offered to adopt them into his famous design of erecting a college at Bermudas for the benefit of the new world. But the club, thinking the project aerial, and having other agreeable prospects, mostly declined to accept of his Lordship's invitation.

There are two strands to this account. One is the specific detail that Berkeley invited members of the club to join the Bermuda party. Wherever this detail is retailed subsequently,[3] it is easy enough to show that the later sources had the *Scots Magazine* article

25

in front of them as they imaginatively embroidered its account; their corroboration, then, is of no significance.

The second and more widely corroborated detail is that there was correspondence between the Rankenian Club and Berkeley, and that Berkeley had spoken respectfully of them to someone other than the correspondents themselves. This part of the anecdote is repeated in some early 19th-century sources with less dependence on the wording of the Wallace obituary, though not necessarily independently of the obituarist's own source. Dugald Stewart in later life published the story on two occasions with different rhetorical glosses. In 1801 he was sufficiently muddled to place the incident in the period of William Robertson's student days in the 1730s; while by 1824, more than a century after its inauguration, he had come to think that the club had been founded for the 'express purpose' of engaging Berkeley in correspondence.[4] On the second occasion, when his language came close again to that of the Wallace obituary, Stewart cited as his authority Professor John Stevenson, who had been *dead* for 50 years. A.F. Tytler's version of the anecdote in 1814 cites the 'good authority' of Principal Robertson,[5] who in his turn had been dead 21 years, was *not* a member of the club, and was either not born, or in his infancy, at the time of the alleged correspondence. But Robertson, like Stewart later, had been a devoted pupil of Stevenson. Stevenson *was* a member, used to cite the anecdote in his lectures, and is likely to have been a common lost source of whatever grain of truth survived the constant retelling of the story.

It is difficult to determine the aims and activities of the club from the fulsome but vague hearsay of memoirs and memorial notices, whose transparent purpose was to make out their subjects to have been the ornaments of their age, whatever their connection — or, more usually, lack of connection — with the Rankenian Club. For cultural and political reasons it was important to convey that Kames, Robertson, *et al.*, benefited from or contributed to an environment of which they were not themselves a part by rubbing shoulders with those who were, and this devious logic has been transferred in the 20th century to the hagiology of Hume. Those who extolled the Rankenian Club in after years as a seminal influence on Scottish culture took their cue from the Wallace obituary, where it was asserted that 'its object was mutual improvement by liberal conversation and rational inquiry'. But considering the frequency with which they recycled the Berkeley anecdote as their

Berkeley and the Rankenian Club

solitary example, they can have had little idea of what originally motivated the club's founders.

In its earliest membership the Rankenian was a student club consisting predominantly of young trainees for the principal professions; some of those added to the membership in the early years were likewise trainees, but as the members grew older and actually entered their professions they also co-opted some of the same professional status as themselves.[6] They originally constituted a forum for new radical ideas in religion and politics. Among Robert Wallace's mss. in Edinburgh University Library is a pre-1720 tract 'against imposing Creeds or Confessions of faith' to which he added the following retrospective note in 1767:

> The writer of this little piece shows plainly how well he understood the contraversy about subscriptions 50 years ago: in truth he and his companions att the University of Edinburgh studied all the Controversies of that time & indeed all which were of real importance with great Care during a course of 6 years before and after 1720: in truth they had exhausted that & many other controversies & those Gentlemen and Divines who have been dealing in these affairs since that time the writers of Confessionals and their adversaries & other writers for and against the Christian Religion and most part of the English Divines seem to be but bablers & half thinkers compared with a set of students att Edinburgh about the year 1720.

Robert Wodrow, the indefatigable Calvinist gossip-columnist of the early 18th century, recorded in December 1724: 'there has been a club at Edinburgh for some years, Mr Wishart, Mr Telfer, Mr Wallace, wer all members of it, who were of opinion that we're in a way of too narrou thinking in this country' — and he looked with dismay on Wishart's removal to a Glasgow city parish, where he fraternized with another student club, in which they 'oppose Confessions, and exalt reason, under pretence of search after truth'.[7] This was the Rev. William Wishart (elder son of the Principal of Edinburgh University), who with his fellow Rankenian George Turnbull had insinuated himself into a correspondence with Lord Molesworth on educational and ecclesiastical reform in 1722-23, writing to Molesworth of his acquaintance with 'Several Others . . . in this City & some other Places of this Country, & even some Few of my Own Coat' who had combined to support the same radical causes.[8] Wishart, Wallace and Turnbull will all figure further in this story; and this evidence that two members of the Rankenian Club engaged another Irish personality in correspondence — though they did not write as a club — gives some impetus to the story of a correspondence with Berkeley. On the other hand, Berkeley's meeting up with that member of the club who did accompany him to America seems to be traceable to circumstances which are independent of any correspondence; and there is some difficulty, once one starts plotting the biographies of the early members, in finding any year when more than a handful of them would have been in Edinburgh together.

I now turn to eight members of the club for whom there is some Berkeley connection or Berkeley interest. Of course, more may come to light.

1. *John Smibert* (1688-1751)

We have to assume that Smibert's membership dated from the beginning, since in 1719 he left Edinburgh for good, setting out for Italy to perfect the skills which were to bring him renown as a portrait painter on both sides of the Atlantic. With the publication of his notebook we can now pin down his first meeting with Berkeley to late 1719 or 1720.[9] Berkeley was in Italy with George Ashe from 1716 to 1720, and they had spent more than 6 months in Florence *en route* home by July 1720.[10] Smibert for his part reached Italy and headed south as far as Florence in the autumn of 1719. He there joined the artistic colony at the Medici court along with fellow Scots artist William Aikman, set up as a copyist, and stayed in Florence for all but 12 months before proceeding to Rome. His diary for 1720 records that he 'receved of Mr. Ashe in agust, 9 breds of fine Engs. Cloth for a shut of cloths in a presant I having given him his head which I painted'.

Smibert returned from his travel two years after Berkeley, establishing himself as a portrait artist in London in 1722 and moving to superior premises in Covent Garden in 1725. Around the latter date Berkeley sought him out for help in the disposal of 'Vanessa''s pictures on the London market, and at some stage got him interested in the Bermuda project which that sale helped to fund. The notion that he was to be Professor of Fine Arts in the new college strikes me as a 20th-century anachronism; perhaps the future designer of Faneuil Hall (1740-42) was to help design the settlement. Between the renewal of contact in the mid 1720s and their sailing for America together in autumn 1728, Berkeley several times lodged with Smibert in London, or used his premises as a mailing address, as his correspondence testifies. Smibert put down family roots in New England and did not return with Berkeley in 1731. His notebook records six Berkeley portraits (including group portraits), some previously unknown, and offers something of a corrective to the Iconography in Luce's *Life*.

Here then is a member of the Rankenian Club in face-to-face contact with Berkeley on and off over an eight-year period prior to the emigration — a ready-made channel for communication between the club and the philosopher and for the transmission of invitations and inflated courtesies. An invitation to join the Bermuda party can hardly have been issued earlier than the re-establishing of contact between Berkeley and Smibert c. 1725, and would then make excellent academic sense; for the active nucleus of club members in Edinburgh around 1725-27 were no longer, as they had been prior to 1720, radical young divinity students, but maturer young professors in a variety of disciplines. And yet this reconstruction is not altogether satisfactory. Smibert's Rankenian contacts had been the young firebrands who had dominated the club in its first years and then started to disperse, and it is among their literary remains that we find the strongest interest in Berkeley's philosophy. The presumption must be that, when Smibert ran into Berkeley in Florence, he had either already heard Berkeley's name mentioned by his own circle of Rankenian friends, or was himself the cause of their coming to hear of it; and that it was they to whom any subsequent invitation was tendered, perhaps even by Smibert himself.

Several early Rankenians were devotees of Shaftesbury's writings and Turnbull wrote a voluminous *Treatise on ancient painting* (committed to the dust cart in a Hogarth satire), so they may have had aesthetic and artistic interests in common; but Smibert has no *known* place in the intellectual currents of the time. He later copied into the back of his notebook various libertarian sentiments which he discovered, in verse or stone, in his travels round New England. These would be consistent with the religious and political attitudes of the early Rankenians, but not with Berkeley's image of the mainland colonies as ripe for moral regeneration. It may then be more than just his new family commitments that led Smibert to stay there.

2. *William Wishart* (c. 1692-1753)

Son of a local minister (later Principal), Wishart graduated from Edinburgh in 1709, qualified as a preacher in 1717, and held pulpits in Glasgow (1724-29) and London (1730-36), before himself returning to Edinburgh as University Principal. Throughout his career his liberal theology, anti-evangelical style, and espousal of the Moral Sense philosophy, made him an object of suspicion and mistrust among the Calvinists in the kirk, who created enough trouble when he was appointed Principal to keep him out of the Edinburgh pulpits for two years. His extant papers contain several indications of an early interest in Berkeley's philosophy which I have described elsewhere.[11] In particular they identify Wishart as the author of a polemical satire, *A vindication of the Reverend D– B–y, from the scandalous imputation of being author of a late book, intitled, Alciphron, or, the minute philosopher* (London 1734), in which a one-time admirer expresses his dismay at Berkeley's bitter attack on the Shaftesburians and his disorientation at certain tactical shifts in the presentation of Berkeley's own philosophy. We know that there was a political conspiracy against Berkeley on his return from Rhode Island, and that friends of Wishart like Bishop Hoadly were a party to it; and it is not difficult to see how those who regarded the whole escapade as a foolish extravagance would be incensed at Berkeley's hanging around London for preferment after he had so badly served the diocese to which he was already attached. No doubt the motives on either side will not bear too much examination, but it seems very possible that Wishart's rather extravagant pamphlet was the final unsuccessful move in a concerted campaign by Whig intellectuals to discredit Berkeley or impede his preferment.

Beside defending vigorously the philosophy and character of Lord Shaftesbury, and correctly convicting Berkeley of an error in Roman history, Wishart was perplexed at the philosophical content of *Alciphron* on three counts.

Like Hoadly,[12] he found Berkeley's account of religious language (*Alc.* VII.8) hard to take. Though conceding that words need not individually signify ideas, he did not think that just demonstrating the influence of the doctrine of the Trinity on the life of a practical Christian could explain what it is that is required of someone who is required to *believe* that doctrine (pp. 27–29). Secondly, he noted with approval that Berkeley in his earlier works had founded the existence of God upon the Design argument, and not upon the mere metaphor of the visual 'language of nature' (though *as* a metaphor he was happy to approve it). He therefore saw the sole dependence on the language model in *Alciphron* IV as a great weakening of Berkeley's theological defences (pp. 32–33). But he read this out of context. Certainly in *Alciphron* the Design argument is defended on a very narrow front: the existence of a mind is only to be proved by its use of language. But these are the terms laid down by the sceptical freethinker, and Berkeley's point is intended to be that even from that disadvantageous position he can beat the freethinker at his game. Finally, Wishart was very exercised by a passage at *Alciphron* iv.12, in which the arbitrariness of visual as of other signs is illustrated by an analogy which shows how visual clues might be falsified by mirrors. (Wishart seems not to have noticed the same point at *New theory of vision* 45.) Once the language of nature is accorded the status of a divine language (and he seems not to have noticed that *this* goes back to *Principles* 44), it then becomes possible to see God as a source of lies (pp. 11, 32). Wishart himself, on pp. 33-35, managed to resolve the paradox in line with the original *Theory of vision* — the same visual ideas are found by experience to signify different sequences of real tactual ideas depending upon the other circumstances, and then it is we who from inadequate experience may misread correct signs. So where was the problem?

What this suggests is that Wishart's understanding of the spirit of Berkeley's philosophy was better than his ability to sort out the letter of particular arguments. He admired the 'most ingenious' *Theory of vision* and the literary skill of *Three dialogues*, and a criticism of Lord Kames in a shorthand notebook shows that he did not make the mistake of many 18th-century Scots, of thinking that Berkeley had denied the reality of the natural world. He wrote nothing explicitly about matter, but saw the substance of Berkeley's philosophy in his voluntarist cosmology and in the support this gave to natural theology. 'He has there clearly proved, that the whole Assemblage of sensible Objects is a constant Production, a new Creation every Moment' (*Vindication*, p. 32).

3. *George Turnbull* (1698-1748)

Another minister's son, Turnbull graduated from Edinburgh in April 1721 and in the same month was appointed a philosophy regent at Marischal College, Aberdeen. After 1726 he became a private tutor and in the 1730s went over to the Anglican church; he became friendly with Thomas Rundle who eventually found him a country parish in Co. Derry. In August 1722 he had embarked with Wishart on the nine-month correspondence with Molesworth, on the hope of rebuilding education generally, and Scottish education in particular, on 'free thought' and a liberation from 'proud domineering pedantick Priests'. Disgruntled in the 1720s with every job he attempted and with great ambitions as a social climber, Turnbull might seem an obvious opportunist to sign up for a new educational venture in America; but his opposition, and that of other early Rankenians, to credal subscription in education would have been a serious barrier. The graduation theses of Patrick Hardie and David Verner, the presiding regents for the graduating classes at Marischal College in 1719 and 1721 respectively, show that Berkeley and Shaftesbury were being discussed at Aberdeen (Berkeley unsympathetically, Shaftesbury sympathetically) before even Turnbull appeared on the scene.[13] Turnbull took the 1723 and 1726 classes through to graduation, the latter including Thomas Reid; but any suggestion that Reid could have derived an early addiction to Berkeley's philosophy from Turnbull's teaching is put in doubt by the graduation theses for that year, which consist entirely in exercises in Newtonian cosmology and natural religion. Turnbull's 1723 theses are rather more interesting, both as nearer in time to his initial membership of the Rankenian Club and as nearer in content to his *Principles of moral and Christian philosophy* (London 1740), a work acknowledged in the preface to have been based on a course of lectures at Aberdeen. This at least was the work of a man who had read Berkeley, though we cannot *prove* from it that he had read Berkeley before going to Aberdeen.

Volume I of Turnbull's *Principles* contains three explicit allusions to the Bishop of 'Cloyne', the one in the preface merely introducing the other two. On pp. 3-4 is an approximate quotation brought together from sections 31 and 151 of Berkeley's *Principles of human knowledge*, about the impossibility of any knowledge of nature without general laws — a central theme in Turnbull's system. In observing universal laws, nature speaks to us in a constant language (ibid.), a language which as regards 'magnitudes, distances and forms, and . . . the connexions between the ideas of sight and touch' we learn in our tenderest years (pp. 38-39). That the idea of Distance is an idea of touch 'suggested' by other ideas of sight is reiterated elsewhere (e.g., pp. 87-90), but given an associationist interpretation that Berkeley himself had outgrown, so that Turnbull is led into an associationist and imagist theory of linguistic signification (e.g., p. 55) that Berkeley would have repudiated.

Other themes that would have been generally congenial to Berkeley include Turnbull's account of action:

> The perception, uneasiness, itch, or whatever it is that excites the
> will to take it, and the moving the hand, opening the box, taking

> snuff between the fingers, putting it to the nose, drawing it up, and being irritated or pung'd by it; what is there in all these but mere sensation or passion? The whole effect, the volitions to take it, open the box, &c. excepted, is but a succession of passive sensations. And it is so with respect to every other active habit, because it is so with respect to every action. (p. 83n.)

Or the following account of death:

> The dissolution of our bodies is no more than putting an end to our communication with the sensible world, or to one kind of ideas we now receive from without, and the order in which they are conveyed into our minds. (p. 229)

There are several places where the destruction of matter is described as the loss of a certain class of perceptions (pp. 232-3, 234, 237, 241); and in Volume II (p. 22) there is this remarkable claim:

> Indeed, properly speaking, what we call matter and space, are but certain orders of sensible ideas produced in us, according to established rules of nature by some external cause; for when we speak of material effects and of space, we only mean, and can indeed only mean, certain sensible perceptions excited in our mind according to a certain order, which are experienced to be absolutely inert and passive, and to have no productive force.

Taken out of context it is easy enough to mistake the thrust of these remarks, which is that there is no active matter and that the only agents are minds. There is a contingent yet law-governed association between our minds or true selves and their sense-derived experiences: the so-called dissolution of our bodies is, *as far as our minds are concerned*, nothing more than the stopping of those experiences, releasing us for higher things. But Turnbull still thought, *pace* Berkeley, that there was a *passive* matter, and that these laws link 'operations produced upon it' with 'certain sensations or passions in minds' (vol. I, pp. 237-8). On p. 233 bodies are called 'unperceiving substances' and on p. 235 'inanimate substances'. They consist of matter, which has a 'form and texture' that can be modified (pp. 241-2); it is atomic in character, so that 'even unconscious matter, in its seeming dissolution, is not destroyed, but only changed' (p. 234). In fact Turnbull had been at pains to develop not just a dualism of matter and mind, but a parallelism of texture, because if something as paltry as matter is actually indestructible, so that death is not even the destruction of matter but just something else happening to it, then mind, which is a far less paltry thing in the order of nature, is even more certainly indestructible (pp. 232-5). He did indeed say, 'Existence would be thrown away upon a material system, if it were not perceived by minds or enjoyed by them' (p. 62; cf. 232, 235, 408, 433-4) and that perceiving beings 'are the only ones to whom existence can really be any benefit or blessing' (p. 233; cf. 235). But this is not an ontological thesis, à la Berkeley, but a teleological one: since stupid matter does exist, there must be non-stupid beings in whose experience it has a necessary role to play.

Turnbull then accepted some important themes from the theory of vision and yet rejected Berkeley's basic metaphysics. And this should not surprise us. Early in his philosophy he set out to distinguish, as Berkeley failed to do, between genuinely *complex* ideas, as of a peach, and *associated* ideas, which 'have no natural or necessary coherence, but that cohere or are mixed by customary association', like a peach associated with past agreeable, or disagreeable, circumstances (pp. 84-86). The former is the idea of a particular combination of qualities *in the same subject*, brought about according to causal laws (pp. 84, 91), a characterization for which the authority cited was not Berkeley — but *Locke*. And the Lockean preconceptions of Scots readers of Berkeley become increasingly apparent as this story proceeds.

4. *Robert Wallace* (1697-1771)

Yet another minister's son, Wallace entered Edinburgh University in 1711 but did not graduate. In 1720 he was employed for a session as deputy to James Gregory, the ailing professor of mathematics; his mathematical skills were maintained into later life, when he made his reputation as one of the first demographic economists and helped plan an annuity system. Appointed to the parish of Moffat in 1723, he moved back to the first of two charges in Edinburgh in 1733. Both he and Berkeley owed their ecclesiastical advancement around the same time to the impact of their theological writing upon the impressionable Queen Caroline, at a time when another former Rankenian, Isaac Maddox, was the queen's chaplain. Wallace was Turnbull's brother-in-law.

From his early manuscript essays, intended for a book-length 'Defence of Religion naturall and Revealed' which never materialized, to a mature address against passive obedience in 1754,[14] Wallace was an uncompromising act-utilitarian and articulate critic

34

of divine-command ethics and of absolute moral prescriptions. Prohibitions, e.g. against taking others' property without their consent, or against the taking of life including one's own, must be allowed to vary with circumstances, according as the action 'tends' or not to make mankind happy and 'easy'; if even the Bible was not explicit in citing exceptions to its rules, like 'Children, obey your parents *in all things*', then the exceptions *had to be understood*. There seems little room for compatibility between the liberal humanism of Wallace's moral stance and the theological conservatism of Berkeley's; but there are still two reasons why Wallace merits a brief notice here.

First, there is a short, superficial paper by Wallace among the Hume mss. in the Royal Society of Edinburgh.[15] It is an adjudication between two papers — of which the second is missing and was probably Hume's lost essay on Geometry — concerned with the foundations of geometry, the nature of the abstractness of its abstract reasoning, and the problem of infinite divisibility. Wallace noted that all three were agreed in starting from the Berkeleyan premise that 'there are no abstract nor Generall nor Universal ideas: every Idea is of a particular Determined object'. But considering himself a straight mathematician, Wallace tried not to be drawn into metaphysics and into the debate as to whether there is any ultimate distinction between visible lines and real lines. The mathematician can 'consider' the properties of figures to be a certain way whether they are or not — that is, can make 'suppositions' for the purposes of a demonstration. We may be able to give an arithmetical interpretation to these suppositions to which we can give no corresponding interpretation in the imagination, and so the conflict arises between the belief in infinite and finite divisibility. Wallace himself believed in the existence of real minima ('the reall solution or answer can not be got till we come to the minima naturae'), without committing himself on their sensible status.

In another and more substantial work, Wallace did more than just nose around a Berkeleyan problem: he commended a Berkeleyan solution. But this is definitely post-Bermuda Berkeley, and belongs to Wallace's economic writing, not as a member of the Rankenian Club but as a member of the Select Society in the mid-century. In *Characteristics of the present political state of Great Britain* (Edinburgh 1758), Wallace made a study of recent writings relating 'to our paper-credit, to our taxes, to the public debts, to our luxury, to our effeminacy, and to a variety of other political subjects', supporting Berkeley's *Querist* on a number of these topics.

M. A. Stewart

> No man hath explained the general nature of Banking, hath shown
> the advantages of Banks, and hath answered the objections against
> them, more concisely, and with greater force of argument, than this
> ingenious author; whose Querist deserves well to be perused by every
> lover of his country, and of mankind.

Wallace could not understand Hume's praise of the lack of banks
and paper-credit in France. He thought Berkeley right to derive
economic lessons from Dutch rather than French commercial
experience. But he agreed with both Berkeley and Hume that money
is a relatively insignificant component of wealth compared with
goods and commodities, and supported Berkeley in the view that
the material comfort of the common people is 'one of the surest
marks of national wealth'.

5. *George Young* (16??-17??)

Young was apprenticed to an Edinburgh surgeon in 1711 and
qualified in 1719. He was a friend in the same period of Wishart
and Turnbull, both of whom used his address as a mail-drop in
their correspondence with Molesworth. The library catalogue of the
Royal College of Physicians of Edinburgh identifies him as having
lectured in medicine in the city from 1725 to 1755; in that library
is a set of student notes on Young's philosophically interesting
Lectures on the Practice of Physic, taken down from dictation by
the future eminent physician Robert Whytt in 1730-31. Some dec-
ades later, Dr John Boswell (d. 1780), uncle of the literary butterfly,
recorded on the fly-leaf that Young was 'a very acute sensible,
honest, good Natur'd man, but a great Sceptick in Medicine (&
empirick) as well as in every other thing, confining himself to
good evident common sense'.[16] Young himself, however — just like
Berkeley — saw the *other* side's ideas as the ones that properly
generated scepticism.

Young has lectures 'Of Muscular Motion' (fol. 431 ff.) and 'Of
Sensation' (fol. 467 ff.) in which he calls in question the utility of
attempts to connect mind and body by hidden mechanisms. The
only mechanisms we are entitled to believe in are those that are
perceivable and discovered by experience to exemplify universal
regularities; beyond those observable regularities any further explanation is redundant, except an explanation referring the regularities
to the will of God. Thus in trying to understand how the dilating

36

of the muscle, which is the earliest observable stage of a physical action, follows upon an act of the will, it is theoretically futile to postulate some further unobservable instrument like animal spirits. And in perception, the mechanisms proposed to explain the 'exciting' in us of 'Ideas' are based on no experimental evidence and generate 'Innumerable Difficultys' which put one 'In Danger of Scepticizing'. Rather, the laws we are looking for are simply those which assert the regular conjunction of nerve-events and ideas.

Although Young is in a long tradition of sceptical or empiric writers in medicine, it is interesting to see the convergence of this tradition with Berkeleyan notions of the nature and phenomenal status of natural laws around the 1720s. The occasionalist reduction of mind-body interaction to constant conjunction is found also in some of Turnbull's writing on volition and perception, although Turnbull was more tolerant than Young of allowing hidden mechanisms in nature.

6. *Colin Maclaurin* (1698-1746)

Glasgow trained, Maclaurin became professor of Mathematics at Marischal College, Aberdeen, at the age of 19 and was elected a Fellow of the Royal Society at 21. He briefly overlapped with Turnbull at Aberdeen — that is, when not abroad as a private tutor — and struck up a friendship which cooled in the 1730s when Turnbull abandoned Presbyterianism. Another minister's son and brother of an evangelical minister in Glasgow, Maclaurin possibly never shared the theological radicalism of some of the earliest members of the Rankenian Club. He moved to Edinburgh in 1725, another in the succession of substitutes for the professor of Mathematics. It is through his lifelong work as an apologist for Newton that he comes to the notice of Berkeley scholars.

When Berkeley published *The analyst* in 1734, Maclaurin began work on a reply. According to his biographer, Patrick Murdoch, he intended both to defend Newton's doctrine of fluxions as a piece of intelligible mathematics and to rebut the charge that it was an infidel doctrine.[17] His fully fledged *Treatise of fluxions* (London 1742) addressed only the first of these aims. 'His demonstrations had been, several years before, communicated to Dr. *Berkley*, and Mr. *Maclaurin* had treated him with the greatest personal respect and civility: notwithstanding which, in his pamphlet on tar-water, he renews the charge, as if nothing had been done.' The intermediary for *this* communication between a Rankenian and Berkeley may well have been Thomas Rundle, who had been active at Court promoting an early draft of Maclaurin's account of Newton. When Wishart had published his *Vindication* in 1734 he had been careful to preserve his anonymity, lest Maclaurin tell Rundle 'who is intimate with Berkeley'.

Of more general interest, but equally post-Bermuda, are Maclaurin's comments on Berkeley in *An account of Sir Isaac Newton's philosophical discoveries* (posth., London 1748). A significant part of this was completed in the 1730s; but Maclaurin continued to expand it up to his death, and the first allusion to Berkeley, at i.v.3, coming at the end of a history of philosophical theories, can hardly have antedated the publication of Hume's *Treatise* even if it does not indicate a reading of it at first hand. Maclaurin there distinguishes those who 'admit nothing but perceptions, and things which perceive' from those who 'have pursued this way of reasoning, till they have admitted nothing but their own perceptions'. His subsequent discussion shows that he does not take either of these post-Newtonian developments very seriously.

Maclaurin criticizes Berkeley's semantic theory of ideas at ii.i.2, his view of the relativity of what is perceived to the perceiver at ii.i.3, his argument from *minima sensibilia* to the impossibility of infinite division at ii.i. 7, and his denial of absolute motion at ii.i.8. Even when Maclaurin's position is sensible in itself, his actual arguments do no more than beg the question against Berkeley — with the usual bland put-down about the things, like causal interaction and essences, that of course we don't understand — and they ignore the passages such as *Principles* 112-15 where Berkeley has anticipated the objections. There is no real grasp of the serious questions Berkeley posed for the uncritical dualism which Maclaurin and his contemporaries complacently took over from Locke and Newton and which they fallaciously equated with a robust sense of reality;[18] and a total failure to appreciate the distinction between a particular scientific cosmology and the metaphysics of science, between Newtonian theory and the ontological interpretation of the theory. Only in Book iii does Maclaurin start to raise interesting questions for Berkeley's philosophy. He concedes a good deal of the incidental detail from the theory of vision (ii. i. 3-4), but jibs at the suggestion that we do not apply real geometry to the objects of sight, in identifying the relative positions of bodies in space. But even here the important issues are never pressed — on the relation between visual and tactile geometry in meteorological and astronomical calculation and on what a tactile understanding of cosmic distances might have been.

7. *John Stevenson* (1695-1775)

Stevenson has already figured as a likely lost source of the memory of a Berkeley-Rankenian connection. Unfortunately, almost everything else about him is lost too. He inspired affection as professor of Logic at Edinburgh for 45 years from 1730, teaching aesthetics and *belles lettres*, and reputedly basing his Logic course for most of his career upon Locke's *Essay* until Reid's *Inquiry* in 1764 caused him to have second thoughts. Little is known of his early education. Unpublished correspondence implies that he had been a friend of Wishart's from around the foundation of the Rankenian Club. He attended fellow Rankenian Charles Mackie's lectures on History and Antiquities in the early 1720s but not as a fee-paying student. He spent some time as a private tutor.

There survives in Edinburgh University Library a manuscript volume containing a selection from the essays publicly presented before the Faculty by members of Stevenson's class. The volume starts at 1737, when Wishart as the new Principal revived the practice of presenting essays before the Faculty; it runs to 1750. Among the essays are themes that were found in the correspondence of Turnbull and Wishart with Molesworth in the 1720s: Shaftesbury's philosophy as the basis for a doctrine of civic virtue, the moral ideals of ancient education, and freedom of thought as a guarantee against tyranny. There are also four essays on Berkeley but, strikingly, none after 1740. One will be disappointed if one looks here for firm evidence of earlier Rankenian attitudes to Berkeley, since Stevenson actually directed his students to the latest literature irrespective of its quality.

So Alexander Cockburn (16 April 1737) reproduces uncritically Berkeley's views on the perception of distance, size and shape, but reinforces them with evidence from Cheselden. However he says nothing about immaterialism, and perhaps that *is* in line with a Rankenian tendency to isolate the theory of vision from Berkeley's metaphysics. Immaterialism is the topic of a hysterical essay by Gilbert Mathison (17 May 1737) and a more moderate essay by the future judge Francis Garden (16 April 1739). Both lifted their main criticisms from Andrew Baxter's *The nature of the human soul* (London 1733). This had been a turning point in Scottish Berkeley scholarship (if one can call it scholarship) in challenging the assimilation of perception with the object of perception, but had a far more general influence in depicting Berkeley as a Cartesian doubter who had never found the way back to reality. Garden, who defends the distinction between perceptions and their objects by going back to and defending Locke's account of primary qualities, makes explicit why Stevenson's class was never expected to see Berkeley's philosophy as a serious challenge to Locke: it was because Maclaurin, whose then unpublished lectures on Newtonian science assumed a Lockean philosophy, had disproved Berkeley's immaterialism (it was supposed) by proving mathematically that infinite divisibility was a property of something not admitted in Berkeley's ontology.

The most sympathetic exposition of Berkeley's philosophy, though the student still thinks it a 'Celebrated Sophism', is by John Carre (16 May 1740). This is a remarkable document, since it appears to show the influence of Hume's *Treatise of human nature* within a year of its publication, and suggests that even at that date Hume was being read in Edinburgh as a Berkeleyan, or Berkeley as a Humean. Carre tries to show how Berkeleyan 'scepticism' is generated. We are conscious only of ideas, but by force of experience come to substitute a permanent object for the idea, giving it 'an immediate presence to the Understanding'. The real existence corresponding to this substitute object in the mind is unperceivable: it is not possible to have a double perception (i.e. of both the sensation and the object); and so we are left unable to envisage any feasible relation between idea and object. In the absence of such a relation, and in the light of current wisdom about secondary qualities and the mistakes of abstraction, it is rational to abandon the psychologically contrived part of the belief — the belief in external existence — and collapse the distinction between object and idea. But whatever the logic of the argument may suggest, it bewilders the mind to no purpose, since the belief in external bodies and the urge to pursue useful knowledge about them are a part of our make-up, a 'powerfull Determination' or 'antecedent Disposition' in our 'Nature'. This final move the student claimed to derive from classical sources, *against* the modern philosophy.

8. *George Wallace* (1727-1805)

None of Stevenson's students so far mentioned was included in the Rankenian Club. The membership effectively closed around 1730, though meetings continued to 1771, four sons of early members being co-opted to keep up numbers. Of these, George Wallace entered Edinburgh University in 1742 and passed through Stevenson's class four years after Carre, but no essay survives. He trained for the law and published *A system of the principles of the law of Scotland* (Edinburgh 1760), a long-forgotten work which in its philosophical side-glances continues the tradition of representing Hume as an extreme Berkeleyan.

> Mr. *Hume*, who has pushed the principles of the ingenious, the virtuous, the pious Bishop of *Cloyne* to their most distant consequences, hath employed all the ingenuity of which he is master to prove, that there is no necessary connexion between one event and another; that no one ought to be said to be the necessary cause of any other event; that there is nothing in cause and effect more than priority and posteriority; that events happen only *to exist after* one another; and that our imagination of their mutual necessary connexion arises from that *habit*, merely, which, from observing them constantly accompany one another, we acquire, of anticipating the future existence of the one, as soon as we see the other exist. Every thing which is perceived is, according to the wild system of this great philosopher, for aught we either do or can know, no more than a perception; and nothing has a real existence, external to the mind of the percipient being. (pp. 7-8)

If Hume's system was 'wild', Wallace also thought Berkeley's 'fanciful', though on what grounds is obscure, and he was at pains to defend Berkeley against what he perceived as the uncomprehending and question-begging criticisms of Maclaurin and Kames (pp. 7-8n.). All this was part of a discussion of laws of nature in physics, before he turned to laws of nature in jurisprudence. Equally unexpected is a chapter 'Of the Immortality of the Soul', where Wallace tries to save Hume from himself by showing that a true immaterialist is committed to the continuing sameness of the percipient being to whom the shifting perceptions are presented (p. 42). It then becomes a question of whether immaterialism is congruent with 'the real notions of mankind'. Here Wallace seems to adapt something from Turnbull:

> In truth, what signifies the existence of a stone, of a tree, or of inanimate matter? It is not conscious of its own existence; but what signifies existence to a being which is not conscious of it? Is it of any importance, whether it have an existence such as is attributed to it by the vulgar, or exists *only* in *being perceived*? The beauty of the Universe, the scene of things, the Ideas of man, remain the same in the one and in the other hypothesis.

> Thus, perceptions are substituted into the place of matter; and men are the percipient beings in which they inhere. Life, therefore, is no more than 'a scene exhibited to man'; Death is no more than 'a change of that Scene.' In the present one, various objects, various ideas are in succession presented to him; but the *real*, the *percipient*, the imperceptible being remains the same amidst the change, the succession, the variety of its perceptions. In that scene which is next to be *drawn*, a new set of objects, a new set of Ideas shall be presented to us; and still the percipient being continue the same. (p. 42)

As an *ad hominem* response to Hume this may lead to a few raised eyebrows, but it suggests a possibly interesting continuity of ideas in the Rankenian Club.

How much Berkeley's reputation benefited in the 18th century from the attentions of this club remains hard to assess. The tributes to their subtlety which have come down to us testify more to cultural solidarity and patriotic fervour among the writers of memorial notices and their later imitators than to any historical reality. Even Hume, who was a considerably sharper philosopher than any of the Rankenians, seems to have thought at the end of *Enquiry* xii.1 that he had done sufficient justice to Berkeley's arguments by seeing them as a challenge to the *intelligibility* of the notion of matter rather than the *existence* of matter, and a whole mythology could have been avoided if his contemporaries had taken the trouble to see how un-Berkeleyan Hume's own scepticism actually is.

What we can say is that early members of the Rankenian Club derived some quite general themes from the theory of vision and Berkeley's overall cosmology — about the character of natural laws, the law-governed nature of perception, and the dependence of the observable world upon a sustaining deity. This they saw as providing a strong stimulus for natural religion, and they did not want him to tamper with these grand ideas. They accepted just so much as was compatible with a more traditional or Lockean philosophy, without following Berkeley into the paradoxes of immaterialism; they tended to be committed Newtonians, which they saw as foreclosing the metaphysical options. The supposed post-Berkeleyan scepticism which they tried to draw out of his philosophy I take to be the view that the rejection of matter should lead by parity of reasoning to the rejection of mind — the view that George Wallace argued, against his contemporaries, did *not* follow — since several of them stressed the importance of matter for proving the existence of minds both divine and human and believed it had an important place in the chain of being. While it is unlikely that the anecdote would have got a hold if there had not been at least indirect contact between the Rankenians and Berkeley through Smibert, there was never any likelihood that they would be part of a mass emigration to Bermuda. The theological politics and educational philosophy behind the Bermuda project were incompatible with the liberal views of the Rankenians; this rather than its financial insecurity is likely to have scared most of them off.

In the post-Bermuda period their interests diversified along with Berkeley's own; where his mathematical and economic writings were studied, they were probably studied more closely than his metaphysics. But if one had to identify the main influences on the Scottish understanding of Berkeley in the 18th century, I am not sure that they would be the Rankenians. They would be the more lightweight Baxter (who was travelling as a tutor outside Scotland at the presumed time of any Rankenian contact with Berkeley) and the more formidable William Porterfield (whose 'Essay concerning the motions of the eyes', read to the Medical Society of Edinburgh in 1733/34, was published by them in 1735 and influenced both Maclaurin and Reid). Wallace's interest in *The querist* in the 1750s was not exceptional: there were two Scottish imprints of Berkeley's work in the same decade (Glasgow 1751 and 1760).[19]

Nor can we do much to flesh out that part of the traditional anecdote which claims that the Rankenians posed really challenging difficulties for Berkeley's philosophy. There is a significant addition in the post-1720s revision of the third *Dialogue*, where Hylas is made to argue that the argument which carries off matter will alike carry off mind. The Rankenians may have thought so too, but the evidence pinning this specifically on their intervention is not very convincing. Something like this argument seems to have been going round London independently, if that is not reading too much into the surviving 1727 letter to Mace from Hutcheson;[20] and more particularly it had recently figured in the criticism by Baxter. Since Berkeley's response was published in 1734, the year after Baxter's book against Berkeley, that must be the presumptive target.[21]

Notes

1. G.E. Davie's article, 'Berkeley's impact on Scottish philosophers', *Philosophy* 40 (1965), 222-234, has been quite influential, though some of the present paper is in disagreement

M. A. Stewart

with it. A more historical perspective on the origins of the Rankenian Club is provided by Peter Jones, 'The Scottish professoriate and the polite academy, 1720-46', in *Wealth and Virtue*, ed. I. Hont and M. Ignatieff (Cambridge 1983), pp. 89-117.

2. 'Memoirs of Dr Wallace of Edinburgh', *Scots Magazine* 33 (1771), 340-344. Long afterwards, Nathaniel Morren in 1838 ascribed the obituary to Wallace's lawyer son, George (d. 1805); I am a bit unsure about this, on stylistic grounds, but no doubt the son supplied biographical information. Compare the phrasing in the obituary (on Hume's 'Berkeleyanism') with that in the first extract under the heading *George Wallace* below. Yet when Wallace himself supplied his recollections of the Rankenian Club to A.F. Tytler for his *Memoirs of the life and writings of the Hon. Henry Home of Kames* (Edinburgh 1807), the foundation date became 1716 and the Berkeley anecdote was absent.

3. E.g., T.E. Ritchie, *An account of the life and writings of David Hume, Esq.* (London 1807), pp. 85-86; anon., 'Literary and philosophical societies of Edinburgh, during the eighteenth century', *Hogg's Instructor* N.S. 8 (1852), 43-46. Ritchie doubted 'the eligibility of convening a literary club in a tavern'.

4. D. Stewart, *Account of the life and writings of William Robertson* (London 1801), p. 4; *Dissertation first . . . Part II*, prefixed to *Encyclopaedia Britannica*, 6th edn. Supplement (Edinburgh 1824), vol. 5, p. 112.

5. See Tytler, *op. cit.*, 2nd edn. (Edinburgh 1814), p. 241n.

6. Our main source on the membership is the 23 names covering several generations, drawn up from memory by George Wallace, printed in Tytler, vol. 1, App. viii. The evidence of older ms. sources like Wodrow's memoirs and the Wishart papers shows that some further early names were lost from the tradition.

7. R. Wodrow, *Analecta* (Glasgow 1842-43), vol. 3, pp. 175, 178; cf. *Correspondence* (Edinburgh 1842-43), vol. 3, p. 190.

8. Wishart to Molesworth, 13 Oct. 1722 (National Library of Ireland microfilm n. 4082). Wishart and Turnbull entered into the correspondence through having some common contacts with Molesworth among the Irish Presbyterian students at Glasgow, and one might suppose a similar mechanism for the establishment of a Rankenian correspondence with Berkeley.

9. See *The notebook of John Smibert*, ed. A. Oliver *et al.* (Boston, Mass. 1969), pp. 75-76. I wrongly cited from memory the date 1718 in *Berkeley Newsletter* 8 (1985), p. 19.

10. Berkeley to Percival, 20 July 1720. See *Works*, ed. Luce and Jessop, vol. 8, pp. 114-115.

11. M.A. Stewart, 'William Wishart, an early critic of *Alciphron*', *Berkeley Newsletter* 6 (1982/83), pp. 5-9. The papers in question consist of two boxes of uncatalogued letters and shorthand documents in Edinburgh University Library, La. II. 114 and 115.

12. Benjamin Hoadly to Lady Sundon, undated. See *Works*, ed. John Hoadly (London 1773), vol. 1, p. li. Both Hoadly and Wishart used the image of Berkeley 'wounding' the cause of religion.

13. The Latin theses were published by the regents, to be defended by the graduands before the leading officers of the university and the city. Those cited here are held by Aberdeen University Library.

14. R. Wallace, *The doctrine of passive obedience and non-resistance considered* (Edinburgh 1754). See also 'A little treatise on Virtue & merit', Edinburgh University Library, La. II. 620/19.

15. R.S.E. Hume mss. XIII. 40. See also L. Gossman, 'Two unpublished essays on mathematics in the Hume papers', *Journal of the History of Ideas* 21 (1960), 442-449.

16. R.C.P.E. Library, ms. M9.19. I have no evidence that Young's medical lectures were influenced by a reading of Berkeley; they were of course presented some years before the publication of *Siris*. I am claiming, rather, that someone who had this approach to medical theory, like others who had a particular approach to natural religion, would find aspects of Berkeley's philosophy appealing; it contributes to the circumstantial evidence for a sympathetic interest in Berkeley's philosophy among the first Rankenians.

17. P. Murdoch, 'An account of the life and writings of the author', prefixed to C. Maclaurin, *An account of Sir Isaac Newton's philosophical discoveries* (London 1748). On the

Berkeley and the Rankenian Club

connection between fluxions and infidelity, see G.N. Cantor, 'Berkeley's *The analyst revisited*', *Isis* 75 (1984), 668-683.

18. The early pages of *A treatise of fluxions* had contained several explicit acknowledgements to the epistemology of Locke's *Essay*. Book II chapter 1 of the *Account of Newton* contains a confused *pot pourri* of Lockean notions about intuitive knowledge, externality, active and passive power, the resemblances of ideas to objects, *substratum* (confused with "inward essence'), simple and complex ideas, and the ideas of cause and duration.

19. The Glasgow University printers added their own preface to the elegant 1751 edition, extolling 'so just and extensive a view of the true sources of wealth and happiness to a country, so many valuable hints for improving the necessary, the useful, and the ornamental arts'. Further relevant background is provided by Istvan Hont's contribution to *Wealth and virtue* (cited above, note 1) and by Patrick Kelly's contribution to the present volume.

20. *European Magazine*, Sept. 1788, p. 158. Another letter (John Colson to Mace) printed in the following issue, pp. 245-246, suggests that Mace was already well acquainted with the Gresham College fraternity, twenty years before he joined the faculty. C.M. Turbayne's fanciful speculation on Berkeley's target, in 'Hume's influence on Berkeley' *(Revue Internationale de Philosophie* 154 (1985), pp. 259-69), is based on discredited and untrustworthy sources.

21. This paper arises from research which was in part supported by a grant from the British Academy. My thanks to Michael Barfoot, Roger Emerson, David Raynor and Paul Wood for supplying some points of detail.

Abstract ideas and the '*esse* is *percipi*' thesis

by George S. Pappas

In the introduction of the *Principles of human knowledge*, Berkeley attacks abstract general ideas. He finds that the process or operation of abstracting and the alleged products of such an operation highly problematic, and thus he concludes that neither the process nor the product actually occurs or exists.

Now certainly part of the point of this attack is to expose difficulties in Locke's philosophy and in the philosophical work of other partisans of abstract ideas. Berkeley's aim is not merely negative and destructive, however, since he goes on to show how all of the work which abstract ideas putatively discharge can be readily accommodated without such entities. The argument here, we might say, is a functionalist one: ideas which are neither general nor abstract may nonetheless function in a general way since such particular ideas may be used to represent many different things.

Is there nothing more to Berkeley's critique of abstraction? That is, is the attack on abstraction of no further importance to Berkeley's overall philosophy? An affirmative answer to this question is tantamount to claiming that Berkeley's nominalism, though important in itself, has no special relevance to other central aspects of his philosophy. And, indeed, this is precisely the answer one would be naturally led to given Berkeley's texts. For, in the *Principles, Dialogues, Theory of vision* and *Alciphron*, there are just scattered and seemingly non-systematic remarks concerning abstract general ideas. The picture that emerges is that the matter of abstract ideas is of no concern to the core elements of Berkeley's philosophy as worked out in the aforementioned books. All of these core doctrines, that is, stand or fall independently of how the issue concerning abstract general ideas is ultimately decided.

Though this way of looking at things is fairly natural as an interpretation of Berkeley,[1] I think it is completely mistaken. In fact, as I explain below, the exact opposite is true; the denial of abstract general ideas is crucial to Berkeley's case for idealism and for his theory of vision. In short, I will defend two theses:

47

George S. Pappas

(1) The attack on abstract general ideas is essential to Berkeley's defense of the *esse* is *percipi* thesis, and thus to his defense of idealism and rejection of materialism.

(2) The claim stated in (1) is just how Berkeley conceived of his own work.

I will not deal in any depth in this paper with the relationship between abstract general ideas and the theory of vision. However, it will be easy to see how that relationship is to be explicated once the arguments for (1) and (2) are fully presented.

I. *The case for (2)*

Let us consider, first, how Berkeley conceived of the matters at hand. First, there is no question that for Berkeley the issue of abstract general ideas goes beyond the realism *vs.* nominalism dispute over universals, and beyond, as well, the question of whether abstract general ideas are needed to explain all or some aspects of language use. For example, at *Principles* 100 he says that moral knowledge is also implicated.

> What is it for a man to be happy, or an object good, every one may think he knows. But to frame an abstract idea of happiness, prescinded from all particular pleasure, or of goodness from everything that is good, this is what few can pretend to. So likewise a man may be just and virtuous without having precise ideas of justice and virtue. The opinion that those and the like words stand for general notions, abstracted from all particular persons and actions, seems to have rendered morality difficult, and the study thereof of less use to mankind. And in effect the doctrine of *abstraction* has not a little contributed towards spoiling the most useful parts of knowledge.

On an entirely different matter, Newtonian absolute space, Berkeley has this to say:

> . . . the philosophic consideration of motion doth not imply the being of an *absolute Space*, distinct from what is perceived by sense, and related to bodies; which that it cannot exist without the mind is clear upon the same principles that demonstrated the like of all other objects of sense. . . . if we inquire narrowly, we shall find that we cannot even frame an idea of *pure Space exclusive of all body*. This I must confess seems impossible, as being a most abstract idea *(Principles*, 116).

Here the argument is straightforward: in order to have the concept

48

of absolute space, we must have an abstract idea. But we cannot have such ideas, as the arguments of the introduction to the *Principles* are supposed to have shown. Hence, the implied conclusion is that we literally cannot understand what is meant by the term 'absolute space'. Similar comments are aimed at the Newtonian concepts of absolute motion and absolute time, mainly in *Principles* 110-111.

There is, moreover, the connection to the heterogeneity thesis that Berkeley propounds in the *Essay towards a new theory of vision*. In section 122 of that work he writes:

> I find it proper to take into my thoughts extension in abstract . . . .
> I am apt to think that when men speak of extension as being an idea
> common to two senses, it is with a secret supposition that we can
> single out extension from all other tangible and visible qualities, and
> form thereof an abstract idea, which idea they will have common to
> sight and touch.

He continues in the next section just as we would expect:

> . . . I do not find that I can perceive, imagine, or anywise frame in
> my mind such an abstract idea as is here spoken of. A line or surface
> which is neither black, nor white, nor blue, nor yellow, nor square,
> nor round, etc., is perfectly incomprehensible (*NTV*, 123).

The criticism of abstraction and of abstract general ideas, then, goes well beyond the issues engaged in the introduction of the *Principles*, however important the latter may be in itself.

These considerations, however, do not by themselves establish (2), since that claim links existence, specifically unconceived, unperceived existing objects, and abstract general ideas. To help see that Berkeley did endorse such a view, we may consider, first, a passage from the correspondence with Johnson:

> Abstract general ideas was a notion that Mr. Locke held in common
> with the Schoolmen, and I think all other philosophers; it runs
> through his whole book *Of Human Understanding*. He holds an abstract
> idea of existence exclusive of perceiving and being perceived. I cannot
> find that I have any such idea, and this is my reason against it
> (*Works*, vol. II, 293).

At *Principles* 99, Berkeley says:

> . . . when we attempt to abstract extension and motion from all other
> qualities, and consider them by themselves, we presently lose sight
> of them and run into great extravagances. Hence spring those odd

George S. Pappas

paradoxes that the fire is not hot, nor the wall white; . . . All which depend on a twofold abstraction; first, it is supposed that extension, for example, may be abstracted from all other sensible qualities; and secondly, that the entity of extension may be abstracted from its being perceived.

Here the term 'entity' is used to mean 'being' or 'existence', so once again Berkeley is connecting together existence and abstract general ideas. In fact, Berkeley is even more emphatic about the issue, for he finds the alleged abstract general idea of existence especially vexing. Having noted that philosophers sometimes use the term 'matter' the same way that others use the term 'nothing,' he says

> You will reply, perhaps, that in the foresaid definition is included what doth sufficiently distinguish it from nothing — the positive abstract ideas of *quiddity, entity*, or *existence*. I own, indeed, that those who pretend to the faculty of framing abstract general ideas do talk as if they had such an idea, which is, say they, the most abstract and general notion of all: that is to me the most incomprehensible of all others (*Principles*, 81).

He concludes the section by relating this 'most incomprehensible idea' to perception:

> . . . for anyone to pretend to a notion of Entity, or Existence, abstracted from *spirit* and *idea*, from perceiving and being perceived, is, I suspect, a downright repugnancy and trifling with words (*Principles*, 81).

These passages suffice, I think, to make the case for (2). There is, though, yet another passage which is both more graphic and more important. It is the well-known *Priniciples* 5 in which Berkeley says:

> If we thoroughly examine this tenet it will, perhaps, be found at bottom to depend on the doctrine of abstract ideas. For can there be a nicer strain of abstraction than to distinguish the existence of sensible objects from their being perceived, so as to conceive them existing unperceived?

The tenet Berkeley is here alluding to is to the effect that sensible objects exist independently of perception. This is made clear in the immediately preceding section:

> It is indeed an opinion strangely prevailing among men that houses, mountains, rivers, and in a word all sensible objects, have an existence, natural or real, distinct from their being perceived by the

understanding. But, with how great an assurance and acquiescience soever this Principle may be entertained . . . , whoever shall find in his heart to call it in question may, . . . perceive it to involve a manifest contradiction. For, what are the forementioned objects but the things we perceive by sense? and what do we perceive besides our own ideas or sensations? and is it not plainly repugnant that any one of these, or any combination of them, should exist unperceived? (*Principles*, 4).

These quoted passages make it quite plain that (2) is correct; that is, that Berkeley himself accepted (1). Indeed, taken together they show that Berkeley accepted a claim which is considerably wider then (1), viz.,

(3) Many key doctrines of Berkeley's metaphysics, including but not limited to the *esse* is *percipi* thesis, crucially depend on the sucess of the attack on abstract general ideas and on the activity of abstracting.

Establishing that Berkeley is right about (3) is, certainly, too big a task to be completed here. But some idea of the plausibility of such a statement can be easily gotten when one reflects that the *esse* is *percipi* thesis is itself essential to many of Berkeley's further central doctrines; hence, by a sort of simple transitivity, we would thereby have shown that Berkeley would be on pretty safe ground in endorsing (3).

Enough has been said in support of (2). How shall we interpret (1), and especially what are we to make of the vague term 'essential to' used in (1)? Here we are asking what the *philosophical* linkage might be between abstract general ideas and the *esse* is *percipi* thesis. A full consideration of this issue will take us to the very heart of Berkeley's philosophy.

II. *The two arguments*

To clear away the vagueness in the term 'essential to' in (1), we have to attend to Berkeley's equally vague term 'depends on' in *Principles* 5. We know the relata: sensible objects existing unperceived, on the one hand, and abstract general ideas, on the other. If we think of dependence in terms of necessary conditions, then we get,

George S. Pappas

 (4) Sensible objects exist unperceived *only if* there are abstract general ideas.

Since the antecedent of (4) is just the denial of the *esse* is *percipi* thesis, (4) may be recast to,

 (5) The *esse* is *percipi* thesis is false only if there are abstract general ideas.

Alternatively, we may think of dependence in terms of sufficient conditions, thus yielding,

 (6) If there are abstract general ideas, then the *esse* is *percipi* thesis is false.

where the consequent of (6) results from the same substitution used to reach (5). Of course, Berkeley may have intended the notion of dependence to be the still stronger relation of *both* necessary and sufficient conditions. If so, then *Principles* 5 endorses the conjunction of (5) and (6) or, equivalently,

 (7) The *esse* is *percipi* thesis is false if and only if there are abstract general ideas.

My own inclination is to think that Berkeley does endorse (7). But I will not argue directly for this contention. Instead, I will consider (5) and (6) separately in the interest of seeing where they lead us. We will see that either one will lead us to (1), though for different reasons. Moreover, the points that will emerge from separate consideration of (5) and (6) will, in the end, help us to see that Berkeley does, after all, accept (7).

We know from the introduction to the *Principles* that Berkeley thinks he has established

 (8) There are no abstract general ideas.

If now we conjoin (6) and (8) we get the following awful argument:

 (6) If there are abstract general ideas, then the *esse* is *percipi* thesis is false.
 (8) There are no abstract general ideas. *Therefore*,
 (9) The *esse* is *percipi* thesis is true.

Abstract ideas and the '*esse* is *percipi*' thesis

This argument is awful, of course, because it commits the elementary blunder of denying the antecedent. Nevertheless, it is a natural reading of Berkeley's remarks since we know he endorses (8) and we are assuming that he also accepts (6).

Fortunately, there is an alternative and equally natural reading of Berkeley's various remarks. To see what this is, consider what I will term the First Argument (FA):

(6)   If there are abstract general ideas, then the *esse* is *percipi* thesis is false.
(10) There are abstract general ideas. *Therefore,*
(11) The *esse* is *percipi* thesis is false.

The First Argument is not something Berkeley would *endorse*, certainly. Rather, the FA is something his *opponent* (e.g., Locke) is *in a position to give*, as Berkeley sees it. Moreover, the FA is a genuine threat to Berkeley since, we are assuming, he is prepared to grant its first premise, (6).

The FA is a natural reading of *Principles* 4 and 5 because it is quite clear from *Principles* 4 that Berkeley is talking about his opponents, those who would reject the *esse* is *percipi* thesis. Recall how the passage begins:

> It is an opinion strangely prevailing among men that . . . objects have an existence . . . distinct from their being perceived by the understanding.

These opponents, of course, accept (10) as well, and it is the thesis that there are abstract general ideas on which the strangely prevailing opinion that sensible objects exist independently of perception depends.

If the FA is correct as an account of what Berkeley is attributing to his opponents in *Principles* 4 and 5, we should expect to find him rejecting the second premise of the FA, viz., (10), in those same passages. A careful reading shows that this is just what he does. He says:

> I may . . . divide in my thoughts, or conceive apart from each other, those things which I perhaps never perceived by sense so divided. Thus, I imagine the trunk of a human body without the limb, or conceive the smell of a rose without thinking of the rose itself. So far, I will not deny, I can abstract; if that may properly be called

> *abstraction* which extends only to the conceiving separately such objects as it is possible may really exist or be actually perceived asunder. But my conceiving or imagining power does not extend beyond the possibility of real existence or perception. Hence, as it is impossible for me to feel anything without an actual sensation of that thing, so it is impossible for me to conceive in my thoughts any sensible thing or object distinct from the sensation or perception of it (*Principles* 5).

Here Berkeley's claim is that one sort of abstraction is certainly possible, but it does not lead to abstract general ideas. The color red and a table top can, and do, exist separately; hence, those entities may be easily conceived separately. The sort of abstraction needed to reach abstract general ideas is of another type; conceiving separately what in reality cannot exist separately. Since, Berkeley maintains, this is something nobody can do, abstract general ideas cannot be conceived. Hence, since it is reasonable to think that such a process of abstraction is the only method by which abstract general ideas could ever be gained, we find that the denial of the process is enough to include a denial of the products.[2]

The FA, then, is an argument that Berkeley's opponents can use against Berkeley's idealism, and this fact, on the present interpretation, is something Berkeley himself senses in *Principles* 4 and 5. It should be obvious, too, that if the FA were to succeed, it would not do just minor damage to Berkeley's idealism; instead, idealism would 'come to the ground'. So, the importance of the attack on abstract general ideas, on this interpretation, amounts to this: by denying abstract general ideas Berkeley is rejecting a key premise in an argument that, if sound, would defeat his entire philosophy. This rejection is particularly important in the present situation, since the only other premise in the argument, (6), is something Berkeley seemingly accepts. It is crucial that abstract ideas be attacked and rejected outright; otherwise, the road is open to a quick and easy refutation of Berkeley's central principle of *esse* is *percipi*. Small wonder, on this reading, that Berkeley attacked abstract general ideas.

It is worth pausing to ask why Berkeley should have been so willing to concede the truth of (6). Certainly not every abstract general idea is connected to the denial of the *esse* is *percipi* thesis in the way that (6) indicates. For, suppose one were to have the abstract idea of a woman. In conceiving of, or attending to, this abstract idea, one is not thereby conceiving of an *existing* woman, and so one is not conceiving of a woman existing unperceived. So,

54

Abstract ideas and the '*esse* is *percipi*' thesis

abstract general ideas of the usual sorts are no threat to the *esse* is *percipi* thesis. To see which abstract general ideas are such a threat, we may recall an earlier passage:

> He (Locke) holds an abstract idea of existence exclusive of perceiving and being perceived. I cannot find that I have any such idea, and this is my reason against it (letter to Johnson, in *Works*, II, 293).

What would an abstract idea of existence be like? Consider an example from another passage quoted earlier (above, p. 49-50). Imagine that a person sees an extended object: he sees a red, heavy, square-shaped table. From this perception, Berkeley suggests, a first abstraction would result in (say) the abstract general idea of a table. A second abstraction would be to abstract or separate existence from the visual perception of the red, heavy table. This is something one can do, presumably, because when the red, heavy table is seen it exists. Hence, existence is 'there to be abstracted' just as a quality such as a certain extension is. The overall result would be the abstract general idea of *existing table*. It would be incomprehensible, for Berkeley, because such an idea would have the *general* quality *existence* and the *general* quality *being a table*. On Locke's theory, as Berkeley sees it, one could have abstract general ideas of this sort. And, if one did, the *esse* is *percipi* thesis would be false. For there would in some sense *be* (exist) a sensible object (the *general* quality *being a table*), though no table would be perceived when one attended to or conceived this abstract general idea. Thinking of an abstract general idea is not perceiving. Hence, (6) is true; the *esse* is *percipi* thesis is false if there are abstract general ideas of the sort here described.[3]

Another way to see how Berkeley thinks of this issue is to consider his notorious conceivability test from *Principles* 22-23 and the first *Dialogue*. If one can conceive a sensible object existing unperceived, he says, that alone will be enough to refute the *esse* is *percipi* thesis. Imagine one has the abstract general idea of an existing table, as described above. Then consider a case in which one attends to or conceives this abstract general idea. One is thereby conceiving a sensible thing (a table) and conceiving of it existing (one is attending to an abstract general idea of an existing table), but one is not then conceiving of perception. Nor, I think Berkeley would say, is one then perceiving a table *by* conceiving this abstract general idea. Thus, if one has an abstract general idea of the right sort, one can conceive of an existing but unperceived sensible object. And this,

George S. Pappas

Berkeley is willing to allow, is enough to sweep away his new principle of *esse* is *percipi*.

The foregoing argument requires the following:

(12) If Locke's theory of abstract general ideas is correct, one can have abstract general ideas of existing sensible things.
(13) A sufficient condition for conceiving of sensible things, for Locke, is to conceive of an abstract general idea of such things.
(14) Conceiving of an abstract general idea of a sensible thing, S, is not to perceive S.

We have already seen in earlier quoted passages that Berkeley thinks (12) is correct. Statement (13) is plausible since, for Locke the theory of abstract general ideas is invoked at least in part to explain how one can think about sensible objects generally without attending to specific objects. But is Berkeley entitled to (14)? One is naturally tempted to say *no* as soon as one looks again at *Principes* 23-23, and in particular at this passage:

> But, say you, surely there is nothing easier than for me to imagine trees, for instance . . . and nobody by to perceive them. I answer, you may so, there is no difficulty in it. But what is all this, . . . , more than framing in your own mind certain ideas which you call *books* and *trees*, and at the same time omitting to frame the idea of anyone that may perceive them? But do not you yourself perceive or think of them all the while? (*Principles* 23).

This passage strongly suggests that Berkeley endorses

(15) To conceive of a sensible object (e.g., a tree) is to perceive a tree.

Indeed, (15) just states a standard feature of what many commentators have regarded as the most notorious element of what is often deemed the Master Argument (i.e., the conceivability argument of *Principles* 23): it collapses conceiving into perceiving. The Master Argument, it is said, thus rests on a silly mistake, one that finds expression in (15). But, silly or not, since Berkeley *accepts* (15), he cannot accept (14); hence, the foregoing reconstruction of the FA, and in particular of one piece of support for (6), breaks down.

56

Abstract ideas and the '*esse* is *percipi*' thesis

This objection, though resting on a subtle confusion, still points the way to something extremely important and often overlooked. The confusion is that (14) is to hold for the Lockean. It is something that would be true if Lockean abstract general ideas were to exist. But, of course, Berkeley himself would not accept (14); he uses it, we might say, *ad hominem* to support the FA. Berkeley denies that there are abstract ideas. Hence, the real import of (15) is given by

(16)   To conceive of a sensible object S, *absent* abstract general ideas, is to perceive S.

If we understand the Master Argument as using (16) rather than (15), then there is plainly no conflict between the Master Argument and (14). There is a big difference between conceiving *with* and conceiving *without* abstract general ideas.

What is extremely important, if this account is correct, is that the Master Argument *presupposes* the success of the attack on abstract general ideas. For the Master Argument requires (16) if it is to be consistent with my reconstruction, via the FA, of what Berkeley is saying in *Principles* 4 and 5.

Thus far we have seen two ways in which the denial of abstract general ideas is crucial for Berkeley: he needs such a premise to undercut what would be a crushing refutation of idealism (the FA)[4]; and, he needs such a premise in order to fuel the Master Argument for idealism. Certainly these two considerations suffice, by themselves, to establish (1).

We can now return to a matter we left hanging, viz., a consideration of (5), i.e., of the claim that the *esse* is *percipi* thesis is false only if there are abstract general ideas. If this is what Berkeley is asserting in *Principles* 4 and 5, then the attack on abstract general ideas is even more important than we have hitherto made it out. For, given the attack on such ideas in the introduction to the *Principles*, we get directly the *truth* of the *esse* is *percipi* thesis. The argument, which we may call the Second Argument (SA) is straightforward and quite simple:

(5)   The *esse* is *percipi* thesis is false only if there are abstract general ideas.
(17)   There are no abstract general ideas. *Therefore*,
(18)   The *esse* is *percipi* thesis is true.

Moreover, on this account we can see the importance, dialectically, of the acceptance of abstract general ideas by the non-idealist: only if there is some good reason to hold that there are such ideas is the road to idealism effectively blocked. For Berkeley, on the other hand, the claim that there are abstract general ideas is the only thing standing in the way of having established the truth of the *esse* is *percipi* thesis. Eliminate the former, and the latter has been settled.

If the SA is a reasonable way of combining what Berkeley asserts in *Principles* 4 and 5 and argues for in the introduction to the *Principles*, respectively, then clearly we have again made the case for (1). Indeed, we have done so in a way that seems to have an added bonus: the SA seems to be a *new* argument for the *esse* is *percipi* thesis, one that is *independent* of the Master Argument. To help understand whether this very exciting result has really been achieved, given the SA, we need to look a little more closely at what Berkeley might have to say in support of (5).

III. *Abstraction and conception*

We have taken both statement (5) and (6) from a passage which begins:

> If we thoroughly examine this tenet it will, perhaps, be found at bottom to depend on the doctrine of *abstract ideas* (*Principles* 5).

Berkeley continues:

> For can there be a nicer strain of abstraction than to distinguish the existence of sensible objects from their being perceived, so as to *conceive* them existing unperceived (emphasis added).

This second passage, I think, expresses how Berkeley takes the matter of abstract general ideas to be related to the *esse* is *percipi* thesis. That is, the passage asserts:

(11)   To conceive a sensible object existing unperceived *is* to conceive (attend to) an abstract general idea.[5]

In the earlier treatment of (6) we relied on one-half of (19), so to speak. That is, we made use of

(20)   If one can conceive of an abstract general idea (of

58

the right sort) then one can conceive a sensible object existing unperceived.

With regard to (5), we need the other 'half' of (19), viz.,

> (21)   One can conceive of a sensible object existing unperceived only if one can conceive of an abstract general idea (of the right sort).

We may, of course, assume that if one can conceive of an abstract general idea then one *has* that idea; so, (21) implies

> (22)   One can conceive of a sensible object existing unperceived only if one has an abstract general idea (of the right sort).

Moreover, we know from the Master Argument that Berkeley agrees that

> (23)   If one cannot conceive of a sensible object existing unperceived, then the *esse* is *percipi* thesis is true.

and the conjunction of the latter two statements yields (5).

The relationship between abstract general ideas and the *esse* is *percipi* thesis, then, with respect to both the FA and the SA, is mediated by *conceivability* of a certain sort. The possession of the right sort of abstract general idea is both necessary and sufficient for the possibility of conceiving of a sensible object existing unperceived. And Berkeley holds that the truth or falsity of the *esse* is *percipi* thesis is itself a function of this same sort of conceivability. If one can conceive of a sensible object existing unperceived, then the *esse* is *percipi* thesis is false; if one cannot engage in this sort of conception, the thesis is true.

We can bring out the relevant points with respect to (5) by stating a fuller version of the SA as follows:

> (22)   One can conceive of a sensible object existing unperceived only if there are abstract general ideas.
> (23)   If one cannot conceive of a sensible object existing unperceived, then the *esse* is *percipi* thesis is true. *Therefore*,
> (5)   If there are no abstract general ideas, then the *esse* is *percipi* thesis is true.

George S. Pappas

(17)   There are no abstract general ideas. *Therefore*,
(18)   The *esse* is *percipi* thesis is true.

With this full version of the SA we are in a position to return to our earlier question: is the SA a new and independent argument for the *esse* is *percipi* thesis? Or, instead, does the full version of the SA itself state what is really essential to the Master Argument? How we answer this question depends on whether we think that the Master Argument requires the collapse of conceiving into perceiving and, perhaps, on certain other matters pertaining to conceivability. The Master Argument is typically represented, minimally, as having (23) as a premise along with

(24)   One cannot conceive of a sensible object existing unperceived.

and from these two premises, the truth of the *esse* is *percipi* thesis, (18), is inferred. If one thinks that the case for (24) rests on the *general* collapse of conceiving into perceiving, independently of the issues concerning abstract general ideas, then the full version of the SA can be thought of as independent of the Master Argument. For reasons given in the discussion of (6) and the FA, however, I am inclined to reject this defence of (24). Alternatively, it may be thought that best case for (24) is to hold that there is something logically incoherent or contradictory in the notion of conceiving a sensible object existing unperceived, quite apart from the collapse of conceiving into perceiving. If this is right as an account of what the Master Argument requires, then again the full version of the SA is a new and independent argument for the *esse* is *percipi* thesis.

I believe that no full defense of (24) can avoid a defence of that statement on the grounds that there are no abstract general ideas. Still it is clear that I have not shown this point in this paper. So, the proper moral to draw, tentatively, is that the full version of the SA is a new and independent argument for the truth of the *esse* is *percipi* thesis.

IV. *Final comment*

Either the FA or the SA, alone, would be quite sufficient to establish (1), that is, to establish the crucial importance of the attack on abstract general ideas to Berkeley's idealism. Thus, either would suffice to explain the relevance of the attack on abstract general

Abstract ideas and the 'esse is percipi' thesis

ideas to matters *other* than nominalism. However, I noted earlier that Berkeley is really committed to (7), and thus is committed to both the FA and the SA. We can how see why this is so. Since he makes use of (19), Berkeley is thereby making use of the conjunction of (20) and (21), which we can express as

> (25) One can conceive of a sensible object existing unperceived if and only if there are abstract general ideas.

We also know, however, from the Master Argument, that Berkeley is willing to accept

> (26) The *esse* is *percipi* thesis is false if and only if one can conceive of a sensible object existing unperceived.

These latter two statements imply (7). Thus, the success of the attack on abstract general ideas is doubly important. The successful denial of such ideas is needed defensively to block a quick and easy refutation of idealism; and that denial is needed offensively to complete what seems to be a new argument for idealism. It is hard to resist thinking that nothing could be more important to Berkeley's philosophy overall than his treatment of abstract general ideas.[6]

Notes

1. See D. Armstrong. ed.. *Berkeley's philosophical writings* (New York: Macmillan). 1965. p. 41. However. compare his other remarks on the same point at page 29. Warnock (*Berkeley*. 2nd. ed.. Peregrine: Baltimore. USA. and Middlesex. England. 1969) sees that the attack on abstract general ideas has greater importance than the issue of the use of general terms. but he does not fully develop the point. See his chapter 4. pages 80ff. Urmson seems to come closest to the views I defend here: see his *Berkeley* (London: Oxford University Press). 1982. page 29. Pitcher hints at what I call. below. the 'First Argument': see his *Berkeley* (London: Routledge and Kegan Paul). 1977. pp. 62-63.

2. This is one way that Berkeley argues against abstract general ideas in the introduction to the *Principles*.

3. A further question concerns whether one could have an abstract idea of existence. Why. specifically. would Berkeley object to such an entity? I think the best answer is that he would maintain that existence is *not a quality*. Hence. even if the operation of abstraction could be carried out. one could not achieve an abstract idea of existence. If this is correct. then we may say not only that Berkeley was well ahead of both Hume and Kant concerning the notion of existence. but also that (given the FA and SA of this paper) the real basis of the *esse* is *percipi* thesis is the fact that existence is not a quality.

Another important matter concerns whether Locke is committed to the abstract idea of existence. Berkeley cites no passage from Locke in support of this claim. but perhaps he had

George S. Pappas

in mind those parts of the *Essay* where Locke talks of the ideas of existence and unity (*Essay*, Bk. II, Chap. VII, Sec. 7).

4. The importance of the denial of abstract general ideas to the *New theory of vision* parallels the *FA*. Thus, in *NTV* 122-123, quoted earlier, Berkeley may be construed as first putting forth the argument:

a) If there are abstract general ideas, then there are ideas common to two or more senses.

b) If there are ideas common to two or more senses, the heterogeneity thesis is false.

c) There are abstract general ideas.

d) *Thus*, the heterogeneity thesis is false.

Here we have an argument that Berkeley's *opponent*, again Locke, is in a position to give, *not* an argument Berkeley endorses. He does just what he needs to do; in *NTV* 123 he rejects premise (c). He is thus undermining an argument that would itself demolish one of his key doctrines. The parallel to his treatment of the *FA* is exact.

5. Statement (19), like (14) has to be thought of as a Lockean claim, not as something Berkeley would endorse, On this point I am indebted to some very helpful comments from Ernest Sosa.

6. An earlier version of this paper was read at the University of Ottawa. I have benefitted from comments and criticisms of the Ottawa audience, and of Alan Hausman, David Drebushenko, Ernest Sosa, Kenneth Winkler, and Harry Bracken.

Realism and Greek philosophy: what Berkeley saw and Burnyeat missed

by Harry M. Bracken

Myles Burnyeat argues that Berkeley's assertion (*Siris* § 311) 'that neither Plato nor Aristotle admitted "an absolute actual existence of sensible or corporeal things",' (Id 3)[1] is 'so far off the mark that the question arises what made it possible for Berkeley to read Plato and Aristotle through the distorting lens of his own philosophy'. Burnyeat goes on to say that 'in explaining this I shall be aiming at larger questions about the whole climate of thought which encouraged or allowed the anachronistic misreading'. It is his contention that 'none of the [Greek] texts displays the leanings towards idealism which Berkeley thought he saw in them', and more generally that idealism 'is one of the very few major philosophical positions which did *not* receive its first formulation in antiquity' (Id 4), an observation he says he owes to Bernard Williams.[2] Thus at the very outset of his provocative paper, Burnyeat generates some questions for the reader: is he right about Berkeley? Is he clear about these concepts? Does he provide a framework within which the notion of 'anachronism' becomes intelligible? Is *he* reading Greek philosophy, Descartes, and Berkeley through a distorting lens?

I first discuss Burnyeat's reading of those passages in Plato's *Theaetetus* which Berkeley comments upon and takes to be close to his own, namely Plato's Protagorean-Heraclitean account of the wind which is both warm and cold. Second, I examine Burnyeat's contention in several of his papers that realism is an assumption in all Greek philosophical thought — even in Sextus Empiricus. Third, I question whether it is Descartes who put 'subjective knowledge at the center of epistemology — and thereby made idealism a possible position for a modern philosopher to take' (Id 33). Fourth, I examine Burnyeat's analysis of Berkeley and the problem of 'conflicting appearances'. I argue that Burnyeat's idealist argument against Berkeley goes through only because he begs the question with his assumption of common sense realism and because he ignores (what ought to count by his own definitions) realist elements

Harry M. Bracken

in Berkeley and Descartes. The central question, which Burnyeat seems insensitive to, is that the entire tradition — from the Greeks to the moderns — struggles to find a suitable 'independent object of knowledge'. Once that is seen as the quintessential issue, then all parties to the dispute are realist. Fifth, I offer a series of speculations on what unstated philosophical principles may drive Burnyeat's many arguments; in particular, what may be behind his claims about realism and his quite remarkable assertion of historical necessity with respect to Descartes and Berkeley's *'esse est percipi'*.

I

With respect to Plato's *Theaetetus*, Burnyeat argues that this segment of the text is not Plato's own theory of perception; rather, it is a complex *reductio* of the thesis that knowledge is perception. He also argues that Plato's story does not resemble Berkeley's in several important ways. I shall assume Burnyeat is correct[3] and that Berkeley, apparently like the majority of commentators, is mistaken in thinking that Plato is giving his own theory of perception. Burnyeat writes: 'The theorizing which attracted Berkeley represents not Plato's belief, but his spelling out of the meaning and presuppositions of the initial thesis that knowledge is perception. The theory cannot give Plato's own view of perception and the sensible world if he thinks he has a good argument to show that it makes language impossible' (Id 6-7). On the other hand, many commentators simply find that Plato's insistence that we presuppose that knowledge claims are (a) incorrigible and (b) of an independent reality effectively undermines the thesis that knowledge is perception. Whether the independent reality requirement undermines the *Theaetetus* account of perception as perception is less obvious. But let it be so. Burnyeat also argues that the perception theory offered in the *Theaetetus* operates on principles with which Berkeley can have no sympathy. For example: 'in the *Theaetetus* it is as true to say that the perceiving subject is dependent on there being something for it to perceive as it is to say that the thing perceived is dependent on a subject perceiving it. The ontological dependence goes both ways' (Id 11), whereas, according to Burnyeat, there is an asymmetry in the relation between the perceiver and the idea in Berkeley. 'Ideas have to inhere in a mind; minds do not have to inhere in anything' (Id 13). What is this symmetry relation? Burnyeat's 'pairings' are of 'the having of sensible appearances' (which I take to be mental acts) with 'momentary states of affairs' (which I, but *not* Burnyeat, take to be mental contents). Accordingly, this seems to me to be a relation *internal* to perception and not to mark out an ontological distinction between minds and material substances. In any case, Burnyeat believes that Berkeley is wrong in thinking that idealism can be found in Plato or Aristotle. Indeed, when Berkeley enlists Plotinus and the Neoplatonists, according to Burnyeat he relaxes 'his own earlier contention that there is no nonmental "other" to mind because the notion of matter is just a confused fiction concocted by philosophers' (Id 17).[4]

Here is one formulation of Burnyeat's *realist* thesis:

> It may be, finally, that we simply know nothing of what reality is like, as various skeptics urge. But all these philosophers, however radical their scrutiny of ordinary belief, leave untouched — indeed, they rely upon — the notion that we are deceived or ignorant about *something*. There is a reality of some sort confronting us; we are in touch with something, even if this something, reality, is not all what we think it to be . . . The problem which typifies ancient philosophical enquiry in a way that the external world problem has come to typify philosophical enquiry in modern times is quite the opposite. It is the problem of understanding how thought can be of nothing or what is not, how our minds can be exercised on falsehoods, fictions, and illusions. (Id 19)

The Greek realist thesis seems to come to this: (1) There is a reality of some sort confronting us. (2) Rather than the idealist puzzle of an external world, we have the realist puzzle of how thought can be of what is not, as in e.g., illusions. (3) Hence 'the monism which comes most naturally to a Greek philosopher is materialism' (Id 19). If we put aside the terms 'idealist' and 'realist' in (2) in order to keep our 'diagnostic' (i.e. no. (1)) non-circular, then it is hard to imagine a philosophical position which is not realist.

II

According to Burnyeat, the record of the sceptic's present experiences, the things that appear to him, are 'immune from inquiry, not open to dispute, because they make no claim as to objective fact' (Id 26). There is thus no domain of appearance in which we find 'subjective truth'. And that is because ' "True" in these discussions always means "true of a real objective world" ' (Id 26; see also 'Can the Sceptic . . .' p. 25).[5]

This provides additional support, and I think Burnyeat takes it to be crucial, for his realist thesis. 'The Greek use of the predicates "true" and "false" embodies the assumption of realism on which I have been insisting all along' (Id 26). He adds: 'Never, for example, does [Sextus] claim that the skeptic can be *certain* of "appearing"-statements or that he *knows* his own experience.' He concludes: 'So far as I can discover, the first philosopher who picks out as something we know what are unambiguously subjective states, and picks them out as giving certain knowledge *because* they are subjective states, is Augustine (*Contra Academicos* III 26), in this as in other things a precursor of Descartes.' Even if we grant that the *Theaetetus* passages which appear to accord special status to subjective states do not reflect a position Plato really held, we can still ask whether Sextus Empiricus introduces a 'break between things outside us and an inner (subjective) world of things apparent' (Id 29), and then gives at least some form of special status to these subjective claims.

As noted, Burnyeat rejects such a reading of Sextus. On the other hand, I believe Sextus does make a break between the 'outside' and the 'inner (subjective) world'. Sextus clearly counts subjective claims as privileged. I agree that Sextus' arguments 'work' only in close cooperation with the presupposition that knowledge must be *of* an independent reality. But that presupposition says nothing about the ontological status of the real and independent object. So far as Sextus is concerned, it might be mental or material. Subjective claims do not reach knowledge not only because of the trivial general thesis that sceptics appear to make no knowledge claims, but also because such claims do not map onto the dogmatist's putative independent reality. Nevertheless, they do possess one of the marks of knowledge; they are incorrigible.[6] The sceptic accords these claims special status by the very fact which Burnyeat grants: they are rendered 'immune' from inquiry. Just to cite an example: this line is from the famous discussion of whether the proof against proof is a proof: 'just as nobody can by argument convince the joyful man that he is not joyful, or the man in pain that he is not in pain, so nobody can convince the man who is convinced that he is not convinced' (*Adv. Math.* VIII, 475-6).[7] If 'immunity' in Sextus means incorrigible, then we have a line of thought which runs from the *Theaetetus* through Sextus to Berkeley. That is to say, when Sextus makes subjective claims 'immune from inquiry', he gives privileged status to those claims; exactly Berkeley's point.

Although Augustine is a careful student of sceptical thought, Burnyeat does not make him the *Ur*-father of that Modern Philosophy which develops some 1,200 years later. Augustine, however, does discuss knowledge of subjective states and even a variant of

Realism and Greek philosophy

cogito ergo sum in the context of challenging the sceptics. This suggests that he thinks he is building on points he believes that the sceptics will be obliged to take particularly seriously. The ease and natural-ness with which Augustine talks about our knowledge of subjective states suggests that the argument is a familiar one. Perhaps the Protagorean argument was taken to contain this feature. More likely, Augustine — who knows perfectly well that Pyrrhonians are not in the habit of making knowledge claims — thinks of this as an *ad hominem* and hence the sort of argument which might actually affect the attitudes of sceptics.

Augustine is also concerned to defend the spirituality of the mind and he appears to distinguish mind from body along lines Descartes later pursues.[8] Matthews, however, suggests that Augustine's '*cogito*-like' passages are not in the Cartesian style. Descartes' 'major purpose [is to provide] a rational reconstruction of our knowledge', whereas Augustine's 'purpose [may rather be] to put down the arguments of the sceptics, to reason, not constructively, but destruc-tively — *contra academicos*'.[9] Yet precisely because Augustine puts down the sceptics in such a variety of contexts, one is readily inclined towards the Cartesian reading: the refutation of scepticism is part of a larger plan to present Augustine's analysis of mind, to accord pre-eminence to mathematical knowledge, to place that knowledge 'in' the mind of God, and to establish that we have free wills. That much seems clear without getting into the question of whether Descartes' *major* purpose is a rational reconstruction of knowledge, or rather is an attempt to establish a real distinction between the soul and the body . . Nor is the logical status of the *cogito* statements in Augustine and Descartes obvious. Indeed, Augustine might even agree with Descartes that *cogito ergo sum* is not part of a syllogism but is grasped in a 'simple act of mental vision'.[10] In brief, one can read Descartes and one can read Augu-stine in ways that suggest they are philosophizing in profoundly different ways. But in that case, one can also ask why one wants the story to come out that way.

When Berkeley 'finds' precursors among the Greeks, one should remember that both Plato and Aristotle have trouble telling us about the relation between the proper objects of knowledge and so-called sensible objects. Is it entirely clear that for Aristotle the sensed object can be said to be known? In any case there is an extended discussion as to whether sensed individuals can be known. Correctly or incorrectly, Franciscan medievals argue that if forms

Harry M. Bracken

are abstracted from individuals which cannot themselves be cognized, then the entire structure of knowledge rests on a material foundation of sand.[11] Whether these medieval doubts about the intelligibility of the (Aristotelian-Thomist) material domain fairly apply to Plato or Aristotle or Thomas, is not my concern. But it should be clear that talk about matter is not so conceptually clear and straightforward as Burnyeat would have us believe.

Medievals introduce another pre-Cartesian difficulty for Burnyeat's thesis. They are obliged to speak about angels. Some medievals take them to be purely spiritual. Talk about angels is a way of talking about minds without bodies.[12] It seems clear that in constructing accounts of how angels know and learn, how they are individuated, how they can be related to space and time, medievals extrapolate from human minds. If dualism is rather weak and attenuated in Greek thought, talk about angels seems to generate a robust sense of the break between the mind on the one side and our body and the world on the other. The illuminationism and innatism already present in Augustine and some Neo-Platonists become relevant for angelic cognition and are extended to human knowledge. Aquinas, after all, faced with the difficult task of considering the form of a substance (the rational soul) as a potentially separate substance, argues for the soul's status as a subsistent on the grounds that the 'mind has essentially an operation in which the body does not share'.[13]

According to Burnyeat, the Pyrrhonian philosopher does not make the the Cartesian break with his body and his world because 'he has a practical concern. His scepticism is a solution to uncertainty about how to act in the world; or better, a dissolution of that uncertainty. Such being his prime concern, he cannot doubt in a completely general way his ability to act in the world' (Id 30). Descartes' doubt, on the other hand, was methodological and not practical. It is Descartes who put 'subjective knowledge at the center of epistemology — and thereby made idealism a possible position for a modern philosopher to take' (Id 33).

Commenting on Descartes, Burnyeat writes: 'It is because the traditional skeptical materials support a doubt more radical than the traditional skeptic himself had dared suppose that they can be seen to lead, in the end, to a certainty [*cogito ergo sum*] which refutes the skepticism we began with' (Id 37). Of course, if Burnyeat is right, what he thinks are Descartes' examples of knowledge, i.e. subjective states, are not given any privileged position by the Pyrrhonians. That move he attributes to Descartes. However, I

68

have shown above that Sextus does indeed accord privileged status to claims about our subjective states.

Burnyeat maintains that it is by means of his hyperbolic doubt that Descartes brings into the open and questions for the first time 'the realist assumption, as I have called it, which Greek thought even at its most radical never quite managed to throw off'. He concludes, 'That is what Berkeley missed. He failed to see that Descartes had achieved a decisive shift of perspective without which no one, not even Berkeley, could have entertained the thought that *esse est percipi*' (Id 40).

III

In another paper, 'Conflicting appearances',[14] Burnyeat goes behind some of the issues I have just sought to recount. In a way, the examination of 'conflicting appearances', the infamous argument from sense variations, takes us more deeply into the 'realist assumption.' Although Berkeley does not appear in the title, his views are discussed in the text. If honey, or so the Pyrrhonians say, appears sweet to some and bitter to others then we must suspend judgement on whether it is really bitter or sweet. In a preliminary way, Burnyeat sees Berkeley concluding from this sort of argument 'that each appearance reveals a distinct but mental existence' (CA 72).

Burnyeat thinks we are taken in by 'conflicting appearances' because we are under the spell of an inappropriate picture of what perception 'is or ought to be like' (CA 75). The inappropriate picture is that 'at some level people are powerfully drawn to the thought that we look through our eyes as through a window' (CA 83). Indeed, Burnyeat makes much use of the claim that those who have jaundice find their visual world tinted yellow. The example runs through the literature. It is as if the disease were giving us yellow glasses through which we might see the world. Burnyeat says that neither the medical evidence nor reports from sufferers support this piece of philosophical medicine, which is clearly all the more reason to suspect that something quite different is going on with this familiar instance of the argument from sense variations. On the other hand, several North American physicians assure me that severely afflicted jaundice sufferers do indeed have their visual data tinted yellow by the disease. Following Sextus rather than Burnyeat, I shall suspend judgment on the matter.

Burnyeat says that it is one thing to hold that the real features of an object 'cannot be among those that are affected by changes

Harry M. Bracken

external to the object', and 'quite another to suggest that the real inherent features cannot be among those that *appear* to vary with changes outside the object. The latter principle is the one whose persuasiveness we are trying to diagnose . . . In the end, I think, if Berkeley or his reader is led by the argument from conflicting appearances to accept the conclusion that sensible qualities do not inhere in outward things, it is in good measure due to the supporting influence of the half-formulated thought . . . that every perceptual experience contains within it a direct awareness of something. Which is to say that Berkeley's rebuttal of scepticism in the first *Dialogue* only works to the extent that an internalized version of the window model is implicitly present all along' (CA 91).

Towards the end of his paper Burnyeat writes: 'the traditional argument from conflicting appearances sets up a private substitute object to be perceived in the very sense of the verb as that in which we originally wanted to perceive whole objects out there in the world' (CA 109). Burnyeat concludes with a quotation in which Dawes Hicks argues that far from being a difficulty, one surely expects that (say) the real color of an object ' "will present a different aspect if another colour be reflected upon it . . ." '

Burnyeat and Dawes Hicks seem to believe that we ordinarily can handle questions about the different colors an object may appear to have versus the object's real color. If there are conflicts, if we see what 'is not', these are solved in terms of the 'ordinary' nature of material objects.

Berkeley, on the other hand, thinks there is ample confusion surrounding the distinction between the way things appear and the way they really are. That is why, in *Principles* § 86, he speaks of this as 'the very root of *scepticism* . . . for so long as men thought that real things subsisted without the mind, and that their knowledge was only so far forth *real* as it was conformable to *real things*, it follows, they could not be certain that they had any real knowledge at all'. Scepticism is a target on the title-pages and in the Prefaces of both the *Principles* and *Three Dialogues*. But Berkeley, in both works, realizes that he must handle the problems of sense variations, dreams, etc., *within* the *esse* is *percipi* framework. He still must deal in some way with a distinction between the way things look and the way they are — but without reintroducing an unknowable (material) entity. Burnyeat ignores Berkeley's account of the problem presumably because he is satisfied that he has made a case that Berkeley is really, and not just apparently, an idealist.

Is Burnyeat right in his account of the rise of idealism in the 17th century? Is he right in finding a radically new 'scene of thought' in Descartes, a set of philosophical attitudes not found in Greek thought? It certainly seems plausible to me that even as sophisticated and well-read a philosopher as Berkeley may misread Plato or Aristotle. But like many philosophers and theologians Berkeley turns to Greek sources with a series of other considerations that pre-date Descartes. There is the Christian and Jewish God, an active participant in human history. There are questions of long standing about the individuation of the members of the Trinity, about human souls as immaterial or as candidates for immortality, about private conscience and its foundation in our nature, and — as I mentioned before — there are questions about angels and their natures. After all, the sceptical crisis to which Descartes is said to be responding is itself seen by Richard Popkin[15] as a product of the Reformation.

Like Berkeley in *Siris*, Burnyeat is giving us a picture of the whole sweep of philosophy — from the Greeks to the Moderns. His larger plan goes something like this: (A) if we look carefully at idealism — and its sub-forms, phenomenalism and sense-data theories, we can discern how crucial the argument from conflicting appearances has been. But this argument works very differently among the Greeks and even among the Pyrrhonians. There is, for them all, some sort of realist base. (B) The radical shift in perspective which Descartes introduces and which makes it possible for Berkeley to say that *esse* is *percipi*, is to subject our subjective experience to a doubt not found among the Greeks. Thus unlike the Pyrrhonians, Descartes takes subjective states as sources of certainty. This is to make a sharp break with the realist presuppositions of the Greeks. (C) Burnyeat's claim about the realist presuppositions of Greek thought is also what drives his 'refutation' of Sextus Empiricus.[16]

Burnyeat is thus presenting a major thesis. It is not about a detail in Berkeley's argument. It is about the very nature of what Hume, following Bayle, calls 'modern philosophy'. Thomas Reid thinks the epistemological tradition from Descartes to Hume rests on the strange mistake of thinking that we only encounter our own ideas. Burnyeat thinks some similarly deep kernel of confusion can be sighted at the heart of 'modern philosophy' and that it can be understood and its influence perhaps reduced by the Greek model.

Recall his diagnosis: 'The Greek use of the predicates "true" and "false" embodies the assumption of realism (Id 26) . . . What I have ascribed to antiquity is an unquestioned, unquestioning *assumption* of realism: something importantly different from an

Harry M. Bracken

explicit philosophical thesis' (Id 33). That the Pyrrhonians seek to bring us to 'suspend judgement regarding the external underlying objects' (PH I 99) rather than to deny the existence of the material world, seems to be a consequence of the non-dogmatic posture they strive to assume. But even Sextus reports: 'Thus, according to [Protagoras], Man becomes the criterion of real existence; for all things that appear to men also exist, and things that appear to no man have no existence either' (PH I 219). Nor, as noted, can we establish a relation of resemblance between 'the affections of the senses' and 'the external realities' (PH II, 75). Or again, 'all external objects are non-evident and on this account unknowable by us' (*Adv. Math.* VII, 366).[17]

I think Burnyeat finds that the argument from sense variations, the argument from conflicting appearances, supports placing subjective knowledge at center stage. The argument from conflicting appearances seems to 'mentalize' the sensible world and thereby profoundly to enrich the domain of subjective knowledge. At least that is one consequence Burnyeat believes philosophers who are in the grip of the 'window model' have often drawn. Given his references to G.E. Moore,[18] I take it that Burnyeat is also attacking the 'mental act' tradition. By that I mean those philosophers who talk about a mental act as the relation holding between a mind and an object. This postulated intermediary between the knower and the known often seems to become the object of knowledge. Sometimes we never get past this window to the world beyond. More often, although I do not think Burnyeat appreciates this point, the mental act tradition is at the base of realist accounts.[19]

Let it be granted that our physiological states affect our perceptual experiences. The problem to be overcome is how the objects we perceive can be said to be independent of our perceptions of them. It is essential that the things we know be real and independent in their being. Sensory perception does not measure up to the realist standard. That is why a significant minority within the tradition turns to mathematical objects as appropriate objects of knowledge and excludes the sensory flux from the domain of knowledge. Mathematical entities cannot be abstracted from the domain of sensible objects. Where *are* mathematical ideas? Do we wish to classify these ideas as mental? If so, perhaps we are idealists. If we wish to characterize these philosophers as realists, and we have seen a plausible reason for so doing, must we call these ideas material? That seems unhelpful. But must realism *either* be materialist or be dualist with a materialist foundation? That also seems unhelpful.

72

Realism and Greek philosophy

Just because representationalism has been getting us into difficulty is in itself no reason to reject it in all its forms. Most everything else can get us into difficulty. Still, the temptation has been strong to take the 'representing' mental act, i.e. the 'knowing', characterized by some intentional 'content', to be an intermediary which alternates as the real object of knowledge versus something by means of which we know something else. Descartes and Malebranche choose the latter, the 'by which' option, whereas Locke is sometimes interpreted as selecting the former.

IV

How does Berkeley fit into these patterns? In one respect, Berkeley is reflecting on two thousand years of efforts to make sense of matter, and concluding that the concept is irremediably confused. It is an irritant in matters religious, and a source of muddles in science. But particularly in *Siris*, Berkeley seems to have in mind that as early as the earliest Greek philosophers, such plausibility as the concept of matter possesses derives from the supposition that it marks off an independent entity. Thus the reason we take *matter* seriously is that we think we need it to sustain a realist ontology where this is simply taken to mean an ontology which can provide a real and independent object of knowledge. Berkeley's diagnosis holds quite apart from giving primacy to subjective knowledge or taking the conflicting appearances argument to heart.

I assume that Berkeley is classified as an *idealist* because he seems to restrict the ontology to minds and ideas. Minds always have ideas and ideas are 'in' minds. As this 300th anniversary makes clear, we are still not agreed on what Berkeley means his minds or ideas or physical objects to be. We still puzzle about inherence, about abstraction, about ideas as universals, about the likeness argument, about his God, about notions, about archetypes. We may never have struggled with conflicting appearances but we certainly must struggle with conflicting texts. In any event, I want to slip by the puzzles which arise in, say, *Principles* § 23, those passages which seem to make everything 'mental', and look at another strand in Berkeley's thought.

Let us grant that *esse* is *percipi* can be read as a resolution of the sceptic's use of the appearance/reality distinction. But when Berkeley turns to perceptual error in the third *Dialogue* he draws his own version of that very appearance/reality distinction which he earlier strives to banish. He distinguishes between our incorrigible judgments about what one immediately perceives, and the 'wrong judgment he makes concerning the ideas he apprehends to be connected with those immediately perceived . . .'[20] With the claim that God does not know things via sense (*Works* II, 241), we encounter a difficulty in holding that God's perceptions keep the tree in the quad in existence when we are not perceiving it. In order to make sense of these passages, I recommend that we take seriously Berkeley's terse remarks (*Pr.* § 65f) about the language metaphor and his suggestion that sensory data are like letters of a language God 'speaks' to us. The 'meaning' of the 'words' of this language, i.e. the conceptual, notional, or archetypal level, is not abstracted from the 'letters' or 'word'. That is the point to the metaphor. We no more know how ideas are related to concepts than we do about how language is about the world. The Cartesian Louis de La Forge (1666) uses the metaphor to the same end.[21] Thus I suggest that Berkeley takes the objects of knowledge to be conceptual, archetypal, or notional entities seen in the mind of God.

. This theme brings together the discussions of dreams, chimeras, and perceptual error with the doctrines of *Alciphron* and *Siris*. It undermines Burnyeat's interpretation of Berkeley if he discusses Berkeley's reduction of the appearance/reality distinction into *esse* is *percipi* but then ignores Berkeley's struggles both to reconstitute the distinction and to provide an independent object of knowledge. That is to make idealism (like realism before it) vacuous.

In this context, if we mean by a realist someone for whom the object of knowledge exists in total independence of the human mind, or to use Burnyeat's phrase, 'There is a reality of some sort confronting us . . .' (Id 19), then Descartes, Malebranche, and Berkeley are obviously realists. Too many commentators on Descartes ignore the fact that the primary domain of clear and distinct ideas has nothing to do with our pains and sensations. Descartes' domain of knowledge is grounded on a universal set of innate ideas, ideas which are common to us all. For these three philosophers, the ontology at least includes minds, sensations, and conceptual entities. Even Gilson says that Descartes' 'realist inspiration is evident'.[22] There is a strand within the Cartesian tradition which is both anti-abstractionist, realist, and non-subjectivist about the proper object of the human intellect.

I take Berkeley's appeal to the language metaphor to be his way of recasting representationalism, or, to be more accurate, the mental act talk which permeates the realist tradition. As originally specified in the hylemorphic model, the form in the object is said to be identical with the form in the mind. The *same* form exists immaterially in the mind as exists materially in the object. The object has 'intentional inexistence' when it is the form in the mind. This representative thing is not that which we know, it is that *by which* we know. Probably in Augustine and certainly among the medievals, this account of how knowers are related to what is known runs into major difficulties: (1) as human and angelic minds become ontologically more precisely characterized, causal interaction between mind and matter becomes more problematic, (2) to the extent that matter is taken to be unknowable, the question becomes more pressing — what do we abstract forms *from?* Pyrrhonism overwhelms the model in the 17th century.

In philosophers such as Descartes and Malebranche, we have minds and we also have knowings, perceiving, etc., which are inherited from the notions of 'form' and 'act' found in the scholastic model. But this time, the material object which the form *intends*, virtually disappears from the model. Malebranche, taking his cue from Descartes' dream problem, maintains that we could have all of the experiences we now have and there be no material objects. As noted, objectivity is guaranteed in the old model by the doctrine that the form in the mind and also in the material object are the same. Dubious about objectivity via abstractionism, illuminationism and innatism emerge as alternatives even before the medieval period. It is because Descartes appreciates the risks of mentalism that he requires acceptable ideas to be *distinct* as well as clear. And these risks drive Malebranche to place those same conceptual ideas 'in' God.

As in both Descartes and Malebranche, Berkeley's perceptual account contains sensations or ideas of sense *plus* an independent entity. That is the point to his use of the language metaphor — to establish a non-abstracted independent entity.[23] The sensory 'letters' are not the objects of knowledge; what they *mean* are. Berkeley has more reasons than Descartes or Malebranche for completely rejecting the material object: there are those worries that go back to the medievals about both the nature and the knowability of the material individual in which be said to inhere; Berkeley also recognizes the causal interaction problems; finally, there is the 'likeness' problem[24] — the sceptical attack on the form-identity thesis. Indeed, Berkeley uses an example similar to one which Sextus employs.[25] With the rejection of the material object, Berkeley both wants and needs an object of knowledge. The language model gives him what he wants: it provides a metaphorical expression of a category distinction between ideas of sense and independent entities (parallel to that between sentiments and Ideas in Malebranche).

It is this reading of Berkeley that seems to have prompted Sir William Hamilton to suggest that Reid's theory is more indebted to Berkeley than Reid himself appreciated.[26] In Descartes, Malebranche, Berkeley, and Reid ideas of sense (generalizing the uses of the term) are correlated with categorically distinct conceptual elements. Reid works out a theory of how sensations trigger off our perception. All perceptions contain a propositional constituent, a judgement, plus a decidedly non-Berkeleian 'automatic' belief in the existence of the material object. With Reid one comes full circle, back to the Aristotelian-Thomist model. The problems of abstractionism, indeed, all the old problems seem to be restored to their pristine opacity.

V

In conclusion, I think that Burnyeat's analysis generates three problems: first, there is the adequacy of his idealist reading of Berkeley. I have argued that Burnyeat grossly underestimates the role of subjectivity, if not in the *Theaetetus*, then in Sextus and Augustine; that he ignores both the question of whether material substance is cognizable in Aristotle and the related medieval debates over the nature of the proper object of human knowledge; that he also ignores both the epistemic and ontological problems generated by the need to philosophize about angels. As a result he fails to understand why Berkeley believes that a significant segment of the tradition can be read as supporting the immaterialist option. Like Burnyeat, I have not sought to 'define' idealism or realism, but I have claimed that he does not see that in the sense in which he finds Greek thought to be realist, Descartes and Berkeley are realists. Indeed, the most basic flaw in Burnyeat's theisis is his failure to appreciate that the problem of providing a satisfactory characterization of the object of knowledge haunts Greek, Hellenistic, medieval and modern philosophy. Thus the Greeks, quite as much as Descartes or Berkeley, see both the need for, and the difficulty in, giving independent ontological status to the object of knowledge. There is no 'implicit' or 'unargued assumption' which disposes of this problem.

Second, there is the question of Burnyeat's use of the concept of *anachronism* when he speaks of '[Berkeley's] anachronistic misreading

Realism and Greek philosophy

[of Plato and Aristotle]' (Id 3). Burnyeat has a very clear picture of the development of the Western philosophical tradition. It allows him to skip (at least) 1,200 years of philosophy in order to make his central point. His notion of anachronism is embedded in an inexplicit thesis not about how ideas happen to fit together but about how ideas *must* fit together.

Third, is Burnyeat himself being anachronistic by his frequent appeals to implicit or explicit philosophical theses? Without a theory of the logic of historical development, a theory of the logic of language and culture, Burnyeat gives us no basis for saying that certain ideas are *possible* at one time and *impossible* at another. To state such a theory of historical necessity would presumably tell us something about the 'distorting lens' through which he is seeing the history of philosophy.

When I try to locate the cutting edge to Burnyeat's arguments, I find nothing more solid than a range of appeals to ordinary language. Berkeley, and others, have been misled by a wrong picture of perception — the window model. Hence they provide an account of perception and its objects which runs counter to our ordinary account. Berkeley has presumably been 'charmed' into this by 'mistaking' the logical grammar of the relevant expressions. Burnyeat apparently has in mind a theory of the logical grammar of expressions which is rich enough to illuminate the logical grammar of cultural history implicit in his notion of historical necessity. I am neither defending nor challenging any such sort of Hegelian-Wittgensteinian 'logic of history'. I am only suggesting that such a thesis seems to be necessary to make good on his strong doctrine of anachronism.

Another interpretation of the appeal to ordinary language as the ultimate principle of philosophical clarification is of less help: the force to the appeal can be taken to rest on a particular version of the language acquisition process. Thus given a particular version of the process it becomes possible to take the 'private language argument' as a philosophical touchstone. Idealism of the sort Burnyeat attributes to Berkeley can then be interpreted as depending on a 'private language' and thereby be dismissed.

Or instead, one may decide that Burnyeat means to let the 'social institutions', often said to be required for language acquisition, also generate the logic of cultural history. That way there is no tension between a synchronic and a diachronic logic. With logic and history unified, one can, as Burnyeat does, treat *anachronism* as a mistake in logic. I remain unconvinced. In any event, Burnyeat seems to accept

Harry M. Bracken

an account of language acquisition (and hence the nature of the language 'game') which includes a 'non-philosophical' realist assumption. It is apparently to the great credit of the Greeks that they did not challenge that realist assumption. Thanks to the same assumption, and the theory of the language game in which it is embedded, Berkeley's confusions and anachronisms become evident. But so long as Burnyeat's own philosophical bedrock remains, as the Pyrrhonians might have it, non-evident, we might be wise to suspend judgment about such textual interpretations as may be based upon it. Burnyeat seems to find that in our common language we routinely 'solve' appearance/reality puzzles. So we are back to the implicit realism of the Greeks — and of Dr Johnson — back to what Bouwsma calls the *argumentum ad kick.*[27]

Notes

I wish to thank Elly van Gelderen and Richard A. Watson for their comments on an earlier draft of this paper.

1. Myles F. Burnyeat, 'Idealism and Greek philosophy: what Descartes saw and Berkeley missed', *Philosophical Review.* 91 (1982), 3-40. Hereafter referred to as 'Id'.

2. Bernard Williams, 'Philosophy', ch. viii in *The legacy of Greece: a new appraisal,* ed. M. I. Finley (Oxford: Clarendon, 1981), p. 204. Williams only offers what Sextus Empiricus would describe as a 'bare assertion'.

3. But see Mohan Matthen, 'Perception, relativism, and truth: reflections on Plato's *Theaetetus* 152-160', *Dialogue.* 24 (1985), 33-58.

4. Burnyeat cites a range of entries in Plotinus' *Enneads* (but neither III. 9 nor VI. 9). However, he cannot intend this as serious criticism because he notes, just before the quoted line, that Berkeley approves of Plotinus' 'denial that matter is corporeal'.

5. Burnyeat has contributed a number of extremely important papers to the question of the role of *belief* in Pyrrhonian theory and practice. For example, see his 'Can the sceptic live his scepticism?', ch. ii in *Doubt and dogmatism: studies in Hellenistic epistemology.* eds. M. Scholfield, M. Burnyeat, J. Barnes (Oxford: Clarendon, 1980); reprinted as ch. vi in *The skeptical tradition.* ed. M. Burnyeat (Berkeley: University of California Press, 1983); 'The Sceptic in his time and place', ch. x in *Philosophy in history,* eds. R. Rorty, J. B. Schneewind, Q. Skinner (Cambridge: University press, 1983). There are a number of other insightful and informative papers on this theme, e.g., C.C.W. Taylor, 'All perceptions are true', ch. v in *Doubt and dogmatism,* but especially Gisela Striker, 'Sceptical strategies', ch. iii, *ibid.,* and Michael Frede, 'The Sceptic's two kind of assent and the question of the possibility of knowledge', ch. xi in *Philosophy in history.* Perhaps the most illuminating paper, however, is Jonathan Barnes, 'The beliefs of a Pyrrhonist', *Elenchos.* 4 (1983), 5-43. See also his 'Proof destroyed'. ch. vii in *Doubt and dogmatism* and his contribution, as well as those by Burnyeat, Frede, and David Sedly, in *Science and speculation.* eds. Jonathan Barnes, Jacques Brunschwig, Myles Burnyeat, and Malcolm Scholfield (Cambridge: University Press, 1982). See also Charlotte Stough, *Greek Scepticism* (Berkeley: University of California Press, 1969).

6. I appreciate that there are conceptual difficulties, as well as philological problems in interpreting the sceptical texts, in characterizing *belief. assent, true, incorrigible,* etc. See the material cited at note 4.

Realism and Greek philosophy

7. Sextus Empiricus, tr. R. G. Bury, *Outlines of Pyrrhonism* (London: Heinemann, 1933), and *Against the logicians* (London: Heinemann, 1935). All my references are to these Bury translations in the Loeb Classical Library series.

8. In their objections to Descartes' *Meditations*, both Mersenne and Arnauld refer to Augustine as a source for some of Descartes' ideas. Commentators often cite *De civitate Dei*, xi, cap. 26; *Soliloquia*, II, i; *De Trinitate*, X cap. 10, 12, XII, XV; *De Libero arbitrio*, II, 3; *Contra academicos*, III, xi, 14. The Augustine-Descartes relationship is examined at length in León Blanchet, *Les antécédents historiques du 'je pense, donc je suis'* (Paris: Félix Alcan, 1920). See also Étienne Gilson, *Études sur le role de la pensée médiévale dans la formation du systéme cartésien* (Paris: Vrin, 1930). Especially, 'Les origines théologiques de l'innéisme cartésien', and 'Le Cogito et la tradition augustinienne'. His review of Blanchet appears in the Appendix. See also A. Koyré, *L'idée de Dieu et les preuves de son existence chez Descartes* (Paris: Ernest Leroux, 1922).

9. Gareth B. Matthews, *'Si fallor, sum'*, in R.A. Markus, ed. *Augustine: A collection of critical essays* (New York: Doubleday, 1972. pp. 151-167). Matthews, whose work is cited by Burnyeat, has written several important papers on Augustine. Cf. 'The Inner man', *American Philosophical Quarterly*, 4 (1967), 1-7, and his paper to the Society for Medieval and Renaissance Philosophy (New York, 1984), 'Augustine's ego-centric Predicament'.

10. *The philosophical works of Descartes*, tr. Elizabeth Haldane and G.R.T. Ross, 2 vols. (Cambridge: University Press, 1967), II, 38 ('il la voit par une simple inspection de l'esprit' [AT IX, 110]).

11. Cf. Sebastian J. Day, *Intuitive cognition: a key to the significance of the later scholastics* (St. Bonaventure, N.Y.: The Franciscan Institute, 1947). See also *The Cambridge history of later medieval philosophy*, eds. Norman Kretzmann, Anthony Kenny, Jan Pinborg (Cambridge: University Press, 1982). In particular, see the essays by John H. Wippel, John F. Boler, and Edward P. Mahoney.

12. See Desmond Connell, *The vision in God: Malebranche's scholastic sources* (Leuven: Éditions Nauwelaerts, 1967). He demonstrates that Malebranche's theory is indebted to Suarez' account of angels. See Helen S. Lang, 'Bodies and angels: the occupants of place for Aristotle and Duns Scotus', in *Viator*, 14 (1983), 245-266: 'The problem of locating mind in a body for Descartes and his followers perfectly parallels Duns's problem of putting angels in place' (p. 266).

13. Thomas Aquinas, *Treatise on man*, ed. and tr. James F. Anderson (Englewood Cliffs: Prentice-Hall, 1962). (*Summa Theologica*, Q 74, a. 2.)

14. *Proceedings of the British Academy*, 65 (1979), 69-111 (abbreviated 'CA').

15. Richard H. Popkin, *The history of scepticism from Erasmus to Spinoza* (Berkeley: University of California Press, 1979).

16. In his *Scepticism* (London: Routledge and Kegan Paul, 1968), Arne Naess makes an extended and profoundly sympathetic effort to make psychological (and philosophical) sense of scepticism. In effect, he answers affirmatively Burnyeat's question: 'Can the sceptic live his scepticism?' Given the impact of Pyrrhonism on the lives (and not just the ideas) of, e.g., Montaigne, Descartes, Bayle, and Kierkegaard it is surprising that Naess, although cited, is not discussed in Burnyeat.

17. My thanks to Jim Hankinson for discussing some of these references with me.

18. But see Moore's own recantation in 'A reply to my critics', in *The philosophy of G.E. Moore*. ed. P.A. Schilpp (Evanston: Northwestern University Press, 1942), p. 658.

19. These matters have often been discussed, but for an excellent account see Gustav Bergmann, *Realism: a critique of Brentano and Meinong* (Madison: University of Wisconsin Press, 1967).

20. George Berkeley, *Works*, ed. A.A. Luce and T.E. Jessop (9 vols., London: Nelson, 1948-57), II, 238 (abbreviated '*Works*').

21. Louis de La Forge, *Traitte de L'esprit de l'homme* (Paris: Michel & Nicolas Le Gras, 1666), ch. x. See also my *Berkeley*. (London: Macmillan, 1974), ch. xi. See also Willis Doney, 'Is Berkeley's a cartesian mind?', ch. xviii in Colin M. Turbayne, ed., *Berkeley: critical and interpretive Essays* (Minneapolis: University of Minnesota Press, 1982). I am unsympathetic

79

Harry M. Bracken

to his 'development' thesis, but see John Wild, *George Berkeley* (Cambridge: Harvard Univ. Pr., 1936). See also the very important new study by Geneviève Brykman, *Berkeley: Philosophie et apologétique* (2 vols., Paris: Vrin, 1984).

22. Descartes, *Discours de la méthode*, ed. Étienne Gilson. (Paris: Vrin, 1947), p. 301. Cf. my *Mind and Language: essays on Descartes and Chomsky* (Dordrecht: Foris, 1984).

23. Edwin B. Allaire once argued that since for Berkeley solipsism was clearly an unacceptable option, one should try to construe his position in a nonsolipsistic fashion. To that end, he urged that Berkeley's ideas are universals. In an analogous way, I am urging that we ought to take seriously Berkeley's commitment to a real and independent object of knowledge. The solution Berkeley suggests is one he found, if not in Plato, then in Descartes, La Forge, and Malebranche. See also Allaire's 'Existence, Independence, and Universals', *Philosophical Review* 69 (1960), 485-96. His seminal work on the inherence pattern in Berkeley's thought was long discussed before finally appearing in his 'Berkeley's Idealism', *Theoria* 29 (1963), 229-244. Some of the history of this interpretation is to be found in his 'Berkeley's Idealism Revisited', ch. xiii in Colin M. Turbayne, ed., *Berkeley: critical and interpretive essays*. See also Alan Hausman, 'Adhering to inherence: a new look at the old steps in Berkeley's march to idealism', *Canadian Journal of Philosophy* 14 (1984), 421-443. Some of the history of these matters appears in H.A. Prichard, 'The sense-datum fallacy', in his *Knowledge and Perception* (Oxford: University Press, 1950), pp. 200-14. See also C.M. Turbayne, 'Berkeley's metaphysical grammar', in C.M. Turbayne, ed., *Berkeley: Principles and critical essays*.

24. In this connection see the definitive study by Richard A. Watson, *The downfall of Cartesianism* (Den Haag: Nijhoff, 1966). See also Philip D. Cummins, 'Berkeley's likeness principle', *Journal of the History of Philosophy* 4 (1966), 63-69; 'Reid's realism', *JHP* 12 (1974), 317-40; 'Berkeley's ideas of sense's *Noûs*, 9 (1975), 55-72. See also Richard J. Van Iten, 'Berkeley's alleged solipsism', in C.M. Turbayne, ed., *Berkeley: Principles and critical essays* (Indianapolis: Bobbs-Merrill, 1970). See my 'Berkeley's realisms', reprinted in *The early reception of Berkeley's immaterialism: 1710-1733* (Den Haag: Nijhoff, 1965).

25. Cf. Sextus Empiricus, *Adv. Math.* VII, 358; VIII, 59; George Berkeley, *Works*, ed. A.A. Luce and T.E. Jessop, 9 vols. (London: Nelson, 1948-57), II, 203 f.; also M. Montaigne, *Oeuvres complètes*, eds. A. Thibaudet, M. Rat (Paris: Pléiade, 1962), Liv. II, ch. xii. p. 585.

26. Thomas Reid, *Philosophical works*, ed. Sir William Hamilton, intro. by Harry M. Bracken, 2 vols. (Hildesheim: Olms, 1967), I, 122n.

27. O.K. Bouwsma, 'Notes on Berkeley's idealism', in his *Towards a new sensibility*, eds. J. L. Craft and Ronald E. Hustwit (Lincoln: University of Nebraska Press, 1982), pp. 121-211 (see p. 177).

Unperceived objects and Berkeley's denial of blind agency

by Kenneth P. Winkler

At the beginning of *The longest journey*, E. M. Forster portrays a group of Cambridge undergraduates sitting in the dark, lighting matches, and asserting or denying the existence of a cow that none of them perceives. The cow 'was so familiar, so solid, that surely the truths that she illustrated would in time become familiar and solid also'.[1] Lighting the matches is not an attempt to catch the cow rushing back into existence; the cow (when it exists) is in a pasture, not a college living room. Instead the match, like the cow, is a familiarizing prop: just as the cow represents existence and non-existence, the lighted match represents perception, and the darkness the absence of perception. 'It was philosophy. They were discussing the existence of objects.'[2] Forster does not say that the students are discussing Berkeley, but the question he has them asking — 'Do [objects] exist only when there is some one to look at them? Or have they a real existence of their own?'[3] — has long been thought to present Berkeley with a problem: if he believes that objects exist only as long as they are perceived, how can he avoid denying that they continue to exist when we do not perceive them? In this paper I show how the problem can be solved. Although I am confident that the solution I propose is the one Berkeley *should* have adopted, I cannot be certain that he *did* adopt it. Yet the evidence that it is Berkeley's own solution has a peculiar kind of strength, because any evidence in favor of *either* of the two familiar interpretations turns out to be evidence in favor of the interpretation I propose here. My proposal, roughly put, is that the famous limerick by Ronald Knox is right to suggest that Berkeley's God keeps objects in existence by perceiving them. But it is also true that Berkeley is a phenomenalist, who takes statements about unperceived objects to be statements about the actual and possible perceptions of finite minds. These claims are consistent because the divine perception responsible for unperceived existence is not mere intellection. It is, instead, the inevitable cognitive accompaniment of the divine acts of will responsible for our sensations.

Kenneth P. Winkler

The first familiar interpretation of Berkeley on the unperceived is that unperceived objects continue to exist because there is 'some other spirit that perceives them, though we do not' (*Principles* 48).[4] That other spirit is God, who on this interpretation preserves every object we fail to notice by an act of universal attention. Some hesitate to accept this interpretation because God, as Philonous points out, 'perceives nothing by sense as we do' (Third Dialogue, *Works* II, p. 241). When we perceive an object we suffer something; whether or not it has our approval, an idea enters our mind. 'To know every thing knowable,' Philonous explains, 'is certainly a perfection; but to·endure, or suffer, or feel any thing by sense, is an imperfection. The former, I say, agrees to God, but not the latter. God knows or hath ideas; but His ideas are not convey'd to Him by sense, as ours are' (p. 241). Berkeley echoes Philonous at *Siris* 289:

> There is no sense nor sensory, nor anything like a sense or sensory, in God. Sense implies an impression from some other being, and denotes a dependence in the soul which hath it. Sense is a passion; and passions imply imperfection. God knoweth all things as pure mind or intellect; but nothing by sense, nor in nor through a sensory.

But these passages tell us only that God does not perceive *by sense*. They do not rule out divine perception of another sort: the mere presence of ideas in the divine understanding. The passages are therefore consistent with what George Pitcher calls the 'conception theory', according to which 'God preserves [objects] in existence by thinking of them — i.e., by having ideas of them in his understanding'.[5] I will call the assignment of this theory to Berkeley the *perception interpretation*, because Berkeley does not confine his application of the word 'perception' to perception by sense.[6] In this he follows both Locke and Malebranche, who regard every act of the understanding as a perception.

The second familiar interpretation of Berkeley on unperceived objects is the *phenomenalist interpretation*. It rests on such passages as these:

> Bodies taken for Powers do exist w^n not perceiv'd but this existence is not actual. w^n I say a power exists no more is meant than that if in ye light I open my eyes & look that way I shall see it i.e. ye body &c. (*Philosophical Commentaries* 293a)

Unperceived objects and Berkeley's denial of blind agency

> The table I write on, I say, exists, that is, I see and feel it; and if I were out of my study I should say it existed, meaning thereby that if I was in my study I might perceive it, or that some other spirit actually does perceive it. (*Principles* 3)

> The question, whether the earth moves or no, amounts in reality to no more than this, to wit, whether we have reason to conclude from what hath been observed by astronomers, that if we were placed in such and such circumstances, and such or such a position and distance, both from the earth and sun, we should perceive the former to move among the choir of the planets, and appearing in all respects like one of them. . . . (*Principles* 58)

The distinctive feature of phenomenalism is that it dispenses with natural objects without putting anything in their place. Instead of identifying the table in my study with my idea, your idea, God's idea, or a collection of ideas that somehow embraces them all — instead of supplying a denotation for the expression 'the table in my study' — the phenomenalist concentrates on *statements about* the table, and treats them as statements that demand no more for their truth than the actual and possible perception of ideas. To say that an object exists when none of us perceives it is, on the phenomenalist view, to say something about the perceptions we would have if we turned our attention in a certain direction. The truth of the statement does not depend on the existence of an isolable object called 'the table'.

Phenomenalism, as I have characterized it so far, says nothing about God. But if Berkeley is a phenomenalist he is a theocentric one, who grounds the existence of perceptions, actual and possible, in the will of God.[7] The difference between the perception and phenomenalist interpretations of Berkeley's views on unperceived objects — provided the phenomenalist interpretation is properly developed — is not that the former assigns a role to God while the latter does not, but that the former emphasizes God's role as perceiver, and the latter his role as agent. The perception interpretation emphasizes the contribution to real existence made by the divine understanding, while the phenomenalist interpretation emphasizes the contribution made by the divine will.

The usual reaction to the familiar interpretations is that the perception interpretation is better supported by the texts, while the phenomenalist interpretation, considered purely as a philosophical view, is more adequate or attractive.[8] This situation is generally regarded as unfortunate — at least for Berkeley — because the two

Kenneth P. Winkler

interpretations are assumed to be incompatible. There is, it seems, no consistent interpretation of Berkeley that is both faithful to the texts and philosophically impressive. I want to show that this is not the case. It turns out that we do not really have to choose between the two interpretations. In a sense, we can have them both.

II. THE DENIAL OF BLIND AGENCY

To see how the two interpretations can be brought together requires a brief survey of the views Berkeley inherited from his 17th-century predecessors on the relationship between perception and volition. Descartes, Malebranche, and Locke were unanimous in their judgment that a spirit cannot will what it does not perceive. Descartes, for example, writes in the Third Meditation that in willing 'there is always a particular thing which I take as the object of my thought'.[9] In a letter to Regius he writes that 'we cannot will anything without understanding what we will'.[10] And in another letter he tells Hyperaspistes that 'we never will anything of which we have no understanding at all'. In *The search after truth* Malebranche claims that 'willing presupposes perception'.[11] He argues that the human soul could not create its own ideas even if it had the raw power of creation, because it would need the ideas themselves to serve as the standards or paradigms of its creative acts.[12] For the same reason not even God can create without ideas.[13] But the most emphatic acknowledgment of the intentionality of volition comes in Locke's correspondence with Limborch, published in 1708 in *Some familiar letters between Mr. Locke and several of his friends.* In one letter Locke writes,[14]

> If you say that the judgment of the understanding, or cogitation, is not one of the 'requisites for acting'. Please consider whether, while you want in this way to make a man free, you are not simply making him a blind agent; and whether, in order to make him free, you are not taking away from his understanding, without which any sort of liberty cannot exist or be supposed to exist. For liberty does not belong in any way whatsoever to things destitute of cogitation and understanding.

Following Locke, we can call the view he articulates here the *denial of blind agency.* It is re-affirmed later on in the same letter, where Locke speaks of 'that judgment which in every volition immediately precedes volition', and claims that 'an action of willing this or that always follows a judgment of the understanding by which a man judges this to be better for here and now'.[15]

Berkeley's notebooks show an interest in Locke's treatment of liberty — the occasion of the exchange with Limborch — as early as entry 145a, and the Limborch correspondence is itself discussed at entries 709 and 743-5. Berkeley's concern with the relationship between volition and perception surfaces at entry 645, where he writes: 'There can be perception wthout volition. Qu: whether there can be volition wthout perception'. By entry 674 he has his answer — the denial of blind agency: 'Distinct from or without perception there is no volition'. The denial is repeated later on:

> It seems to me that Will & understanding Volitions & ideas cannot be severed, that either cannot be possibly without the other. (entry 841)

> Some Ideas or other I must have so long as I exist or Will. But no one Idea or sort of Ideas is essential. (entry 842)

The most dramatic endorsement of the denial of blind agency, one that will play an important role in my later argument, comes at entry 812: 'The propertys of all things are in God i.e. there is in the Deity Understanding as well as Will. He is no Blind agent & in truth a blind Agent is a Contradiction.' Locke's own denial of blind agency may well have influenced this entry. At entry 708, which immediately precedes the first entry referring to the Limborch correspondence, Berkeley writes that 'The will & the Understanding may very well be thought two distinct beings'. Entry 743, the second to refer to the correspondence, reads,

> Locke to Limborch etc. Talk of Judicium Intellectus preceding the Volition I think Judicium includes Volition I can by no means distinguish these Judicium, Intellectus, indifferentia, Uneasiness so many things accompanying or preceding every Volition as e.g. the motion of my hand.

Here Berkeley is not disputing Locke's denial of blind agency, though he is unhappy with Locke's suggestion that judgment and volition — because the one precedes the other — are distinct. On Berkeley's view volition *involves* or *presupposes* perception; every volition has an object, content, or specification, and it is this object or specification that differentiates between my willing one thing and my willing something else. To deny blind agency is not to claim

85

that a volition must always follow a perception or judgment *in time*, but merely to insist that volition, like perception and judgment themselves, is intentional. Berkeley's emphasis on the intentionality of volition is closely connected with the view of the relationship between the understanding and will as faculties that emerges on the penultimate page of the *Commentaries:*

> I must not say the Will & Understanding are all one but that they are both Abstract Ideas i.e. none at all. they not being even ratione different from the Spirit, Qua faculties, or Active. (entry 871)

As Berkeley writes at *Principles* 27, 'a spirit is one simple, undivided, active being: as it perceives ideas, it is called the *understanding*, and as it produces or otherwise operates about them, it is called the *will*'.[16]

We can conclude from our survey of Berkeley's predecessors, and from his notebook entries on volition and perception, that in the *Philosophical commentaries* Berkeley denies blind agency, and in doing so affirms a commonplace of 17th-century philosophy of mind. It is, in fact, difficult to locate a philosopher or theologian studied by Berkeley who did *not* deny blind agency. The denial is issued by William King (referred to at entries 142 and 159) and also by John Sergeant (referred to at entry 840). It is also issued by John Norris.[17] The denial of blind agency will be the central principle in my interpretation of Berkeley on unperceived objects. I want to emphasize not only the fact that Berkeley issues the denial in his notebooks, but also its commonplace character, because Berkeley does not make the denial explicit in either the *Principles* or the *Dialogues*. It fails to appear, though, not because he abandons it, but because he takes it for granted. The denial reappears in works published after the *Dialogues*. In a remark reminiscent of entry 743 on the Limborch correspondence, Berkeley's spokesman Euphranor proclaims at *Alciphron* VII 18 that 'I cannot discern nor abstract the decree of the judgment from the command of the will' (*Works* III, p. 314). At *Siris* 254 Berkeley writes,

> And it must be owned that, as faculties are multiplied by philosophers according to their operations, the will may be distinguished from the intellect. But it will not therefore follow that the Will which operates in the course of nature is not conducted and applied by intellect, although it be granted that neither will understands, nor intellect wills.

Unperceived objects and Berkeley's denial of blind agency

He repeats the point at *Siris* 322.

> Now although, in our conception, *vis*, or spirit, might be distinguished from mind, it would not thence follow that it acts blindly or without mind, or that it is not closely connected with intellect.

Although it is not stated in either the *Principles* or the *Dialogues*, the denial of blind agency illuminates many passages in both works.[18] For example, it can help us understand some of the texts Jonathan Bennett points to in support of his contention that Berkeley conflates causation and inherence. Bennett identifies eight occasions on which Berkeley uses 'depend' or related words 'to say something about the ownership of ideas', and eight other occasions on which he uses them 'in discussing what causes ideas to be had by minds'.[19] He then accuses Berkeley of exploiting the ambiguity in the following passage, where Berkeley presents what Bennett calls the 'continuity argument' for the existence of God.[20]

> PHILONOUS. When I deny sensible things an existence out of the mind, I do not mean my mind in particular, but all minds. Now it is plain they have an existence exterior to my mind, since I find them by experience to be independent of it. There is therefore some other mind wherein they exist, during the intervals between the times of my perceiving them: as likewise they did before my birth, and would do after my annihilation. (Third Dialogue, *Works* II, pp. 230-1)

Bennett writes,[21]

> The last two sentences of this, I suggest, exploit the ambiguity of 'independent'. Berkeley takes the premiss that some ideas are independent of (not caused by) my mind, muddles himself into treating it as the premiss that some ideas are independent of (not owned by) my mind, and so infers that some mind has ideas when I do not. How else could we explain his saying that 'I find by experience' that some ideas are 'exterior' to my mind in a sense which implies their existing 'during the intervals between the times of my perceiving them'. The mistake is a bad one anyway; but my diagnosis shows how it could represent not childish incompetence but rather Berkeley's falling into a trap laid by his own terminology.

But there is no muddle, no mistake, and no entrapment. Philonous's premiss is that I am not the cause of my ideas. His conclusion is that they exist in another mind, and his reasoning (suppressed, I suggest, because he finds it so obvious) turns on the denial of blind agency. My ideas must have *some* cause, that cause can only be a spirit, and it therefore follows, by virtue of the denial of blind agency, that the spirit must itself have the ideas it causes, because unless it had them, it could not bring them about. Their existence in the mind of that spirit 'during the intervals between the times of my perceiving them' is taken to follow from their continuous existence: the mind that maintains them must (by the denial of blind agency) be aware of them at every moment of their lives. That this reading does not impute a concern with God's will that is foreign to the passage is made clear by the way the passage ends, in lines Bennett omits from his quotation; 'And as the same is true', Philonous continues, 'with regard to all other finite created spirits; it necessarily follows, there is an *omnipresent eternal Mind*, which knows and comprehends all things, and *exhibits* [my emphasis] them to our view in such a manner, and according to such rules as he himself hath *ordained* [my emphasis again], and are by us termed the *Laws of Nature*' (*Works* II, p. 231).

Bennett is at the very least hasty in supposing that there is no other explanation for Berkeley's inference than the muddle he attributes to him. But are there grounds for preferring my reading over Bennett's, beyond a desire to see Berkeley as subtle rather than confused? My reading is clinched, it seems to me, by some of the passages in which Berkeley presents what Bennett calls the 'passivity argument' for the existence of God, which differs from the continuity argument in appealing, according to Bennett, not to the continued existence of unperceived objects, but to the fact that 'my ideas of sense come into my mind without being caused to do so by any act of my will'.[22] At *Principles* 29, for example, Berkeley says that because ideas of sense 'have not a . . . dependence on my will,' there must be 'some other will or spirit that produces them'. In the following section that will or spirit is identified with God. In this case Bennett is not tempted to say that Berkeley exploits an ambiguity. According to Bennett's own compilation, the word 'dependence' here has its causal sense; the argument turns on the premiss that an idea that is not caused by me must be caused by another spirit. Now consider the following passage, which Bennett regards as 'the clearest possible presentation of the passivity argument'.[23]

> PHILONOUS. Nor is it less plain that these ideas or things by me perceived, either themselves or their archetypes, exist independently of my mind, since I know myself not to be their author, it being out of my power to determine at pleasure, what particular ideas I shall be affected with upon opening my eyes or ears. They must therefore

exist in some other mind, whose will it is they should be exhibited to me. (Second Dialogue, *Works* II, pp. 214-15)

Does Berkeley exploit the ambiguity of 'independently' here? Again, Bennett says no; the sense of 'independently' is purely causal.[24] But this version of the passivity argument goes beyond the one at *Principles* 29 — which concludes that there is a spirit who *causes* my ideas of sense — in claiming that my ideas of their archetypes 'exist in some other mind'. Bennett is surely right to refrain from saying that Berkeley derives this further conclusion by exploiting the ambiguity of 'independently'. But then how does he do it? The answer, of course, is that he exploits the denial of blind agency. Insofar as the present argument duplicates *Principles* 29, it establishes the existence of an external spirit that is the cause of ideas of sense. It can go beyond *Principles* 29 only by committing the same mistake Bennett finds in the continuity argument (and fails to find here), or by appealing to the denial of blind agency. So even Bennett needs to attribute the denial to Berkeley. Why not say, then, that the denial is at work even in the so-called continuity argument? Bennett might reply that the two arguments are very different. But if we look closely at the continuity argument, the only difference we find there is that the ideas or objects in 'some other mind' are said to exist 'during the intervals between the times of my perceiving them'. Now if Berkeley can derive the *existence* of ideas in another mind without exploiting the ambiguity of 'depend', surely he can derive their *continued* existence without exploiting it. *The ambiguity of 'depend' has nothing in particular to do with* continuous *existence*.

At one time I thought that the inference to continuous existence in the mind of God could be secured by the immutability of the mind in which ideas or objects have (by the passivity argument) been proven to reside. But this runs the risk of proving too much: if it is God's immutability that insures continuity, how is it possible for an object to arise and perish?[25] I now think the inference turns on Berkeley's assumption that objects exist when we do not perceive them. (Bennett follows the traditional line of interpretation when he includes this assumption in his reconstruction of Berkeley's argument.) What needs explaining is Berkeley's conclusion that these objects are continuously perceived by the spirit responsible for ideas of sense. The denial of blind agency tells us that the spirit responsible for the continuous existence of objects must be aware of their continuous existence, but the step from *awareness of continuous existence* to *continuous awareness of existence* is not in general a valid one.

Kenneth P. Winkler

If we can speak of Berkeley's God as a being who exists at every moment rather than as a being who is outside of time altogether (as Berkeley himself often does, despite his official view that succession *constitutes* time (*Works* II, p. 293), which presumably entails the atemporality of any being in whom there is no succession), then the step might be secured in this one case at least by an appeal to God's immutability. If there is no change, variation, or succession in God (*Works* II, p. 293) then he must be aware at every moment of all of his standing intentions. But once again we run the risk of proving too much: God will be aware in the 20th century (thanks to his invariable awareness of all of his decrees) of things that went out of existence in the 18th. In the following section I will explain how Berkeley distinguishes between God's perception of the merely possible and his perception of the actual, where 'the actual' embraces the past and the future as well as the present. But I do not think that Berkeley provides a way of distinguishing between the kind of perception God has of actual objects *at the time of their existence* and the kind of perception he has of those objects before they come to be or after they pass away. To put the point another way, Berkeley provides no way of understanding how the limited lifespans of actual objects are represented in God's intentions. I do not think this shortcoming can easily be remedied. But I do not think this counts against my criticism of Bennett, whose own interpretation is no better equipped to solve the present problem. It is clear, I think, that Bennett's evidence for the alleged inflation of causation and inherence is insufficient. It is also clear that both the passivity argument and the continuity argument are causal, and that both depend on the denial of blind agency. In view of this I think it can be said that the continuity argument, far from constituting an independent argument for the existence of God, is simply a modification or elaboration of the passivity argument, or an adaptation of the passivity argument to the problem of intermittency (as the context of its appearance on pp. 230-1 suggests). The passivity argument establishes the existence of God, and the continuity argument merely adds that God continues to perceive whatever continues to exist when we do not perceive it.

It is, incidentally, no objection to my reading that it attributes to Philonous the view that the cause of my ideas has the same ideas I have. In the Third Dialogue, Philonous endorses a 'vulgar' use of 'same' which allows exactly this (*Works* II, pp. 247-8). Anyone unwilling to say that the same idea can exist in different minds is free to speak of ideas 'or their archetypes' existing in the mind of

God, as Philonous does at the beginning of the passage on pp. 214-15.

I hope that my defense of Berkeley against Bennett establishes the interpretative power of the denial of blind agency, even for the understanding of passages in which it is not explicit. I turn now to the problem of unperceived objects.

III. UNPERCEIVED OBJECTS

I begin with what Pitcher sees as the main fault of the perception interpretation, considered as a philosophical view.[26]

> I have to remark that I think the doctrine is by no means an attractive one. Anyone who wants to, or does, believe that objects continue to exist when no finite creature is observing them — and this includes at least all of mankind who are sane — should not be satisfied with the statement that they merely continue to exist in God's mind. It is, in the first place, little more than a bad joke to claim that a thing exists simply in virtue of the fact that someone has an idea of it in his understanding — i.e., is thinking of it. . . . The weakness of Berkeley's position can be seen, too, if we remember that God must have ideas of all possible worlds in His mind, in addition to ideas of this actual world. The kind of existence that Berkeley accords to unperceived objects of this world, then, is precisely the kind that objects in merely possible, but non-actual worlds, have — e.g., the kind and amount that a purple man with three heads has. No one, I say, should be satisfied with so little.

Pitcher thinks that according to Berkeley, 'God preserves [objects] in existence by thinking of them — i.e., by having ideas of them in his understanding'. He does not suppose that Berkeley thinks the existence so preserved is 'the usual, first-class kind of existence that belongs to things that are actually perceived'[27] (Pitcher cites *Commentaries* 473, where Berkeley confesses — though in a different context — that he uses the word 'existence' in 'a larger sense than ordinary'), but he does imply that Berkeley regards this second-class kind of existence as enough to satisfy someone who believes in the existence of unperceived objects. Otherwise there would be no 'bad joke', and Pitcher's claim that 'no one . . . should be satisfied with so little' would not be a criticism of Berkeley.

Pitcher's objection uncovers, I think, the real motivation behind the view that Berkeley's God must perceive in some way that resembles perception by sense. Because God is aware of all possible objects as well as all actual ones, merely being thought of by God cannot be sufficient for the real existence of an object. If divine perception is going to establish real existence, it seems that God has to *register* or somehow *respond* to actual existence — but this is exactly what he cannot do. Any form of awareness that 'waits on' its object is incompatible with God's omnipotence.

If we examine the passages Pitcher offers in support of the perception interpretation, though, we find no evidence that Berkeley thinks merely being thought of by God is sufficient for existence in any sense strong enough to impress or satisfy those who believe in the existence of unperceived objects. Pitcher presents nine selections from the *Dialogues* which, he thinks, support his view.[28] We can divide the selections into two groups. The following passage is typical of the first:

> PHILONOUS. Mark it well; I do not say, I see things by perceiving that which represents them in the intelligible substance of God. This I do not understand; but I say, the things by me perceived are known by the understanding, and produced by the will, of an infinite spirit. (Second Dialogue, *Works* II, p. 215)

The remaining passages in the first group are the passivity argument in the Second Dialogue (*Works* II, pp. 214-15, discussed above in connection with Bennett), and the completion of the continuity argument (Third Dialogue, *Works* II, p. 231, quoted above on p.87). What unites all three is that they make reference not only to God's understanding, but to his will. The passivity argument concludes that ideas 'must . . . exist in some other mind, whose *will* it is they should be exhibited to me'; 'there is an *omnipresent eternal Mind*', runs the completion of the continuity argument, 'which knows and comprehends all things, and *exhibits* them to our view in such a manner, and according to such rules as he himself hath *ordained*'. The vocabulary of volition I have emphasized in quoting these passages — 'will', 'exhibits', 'ordained', and in the passage on p. 215, 'produced by the will' — makes them completely unsuitable as evidence for the perception interpretation. Instead of saying that merely being thought of by God is sufficient for existence, the passages in the first group suggest just the opposite.

The six passages in the second group say nothing about God as the cause of our ideas, but they still fail to support the perception interpretation. The following passages are typical.

> PHILONOUS. . . . Besides, is there no difference between saying, *there is a God, therefore he perceives all things:* and saying, *sensible things do really exist: and if they really exist, they are necessarily perceived by an infinite*

> *mind: therefore there is an infinite mind, or God.* This furnishes you with a direct and immediate demonstration, from a most evident principle, of the *being of a God.* (Second Dialogue, *Works* II, p. 212)

> PHILONOUS. . . . every unthinking being is necessarily, and from the very nature of its existence, perceived by some mind; if not by any finite created mind, yet certainly by the infinite mind of God. . . . (Third Dialogue, *Works* II, p. 236)

These passages say not only that God perceives all things, but that divine perception is a necessary condition of real existence. They do not, however, say that it is a sufficient condition. It might be replied that they strongly suggest it, but even if they do, we cannot conclude that according to Berkeley, merely being thought of by God is sufficient for real existence. It may be that the divine perception sufficient for existence is not mere intellection, but the perception which, according to the denial of blind agency, must accompany every act of will.

None of the nine passages from the *Dialogues* is a response to the objection that in Berkeley's world, objects lead an intermittent life, life, and because it is in Berkeley's response to that objection that we would expect to find the strongest support for the perception interpretation, it is natural to turn to *Principles* 45-8, the only place in Berkeley's writings where the intermittency objection is discussed. Berkeley's responses to the objection are carefully graded. First he challenges the reader to conceive of an idea or archetype existing without the mind (§45). He then observes that received principles are 'chargeable with [the same] pretended absurdities' (§46), maintaining that even if matter exists, it will follow from received principles that particular bodies do not exist when unperceived (§47). At §48 he writes,

> If we consider it, the objection proposed in *Sect.* 45 will not be found reasonably charged on the principles we have premised, so as in truth to make any objection at all against our notions. For though we hold indeed the objects of sense to be nothing else but ideas which cannot exist unperceived; yet we may not hence conclude they have no existence except only while they are perceived by us, since there may be some other spirit that perceives them, though we do not.

Several commentators have remarked on Berkeley's cageyness here: he does not say that there definitely *is* another spirit that perceives things when we don't, only that there *may* be one. I think the cageyness is due not to any doubt that God perceives all things, but to doubts about the position that the perception interpretation

Kenneth P. Winkler

would have us ascribe to him. Berkeley obviously wants to meet the intermittency objection in the most economical way; this is typical of his dialectical style. He grants that things exist only if they are perceived, but he does not think it follows from this that they exist only if they are perceived *by us*. This is because *being perceived* does not entail being perceived *by us*, and to point out that the entailment fails Berkeley has to say no more than that there *may* be some other spirit that perceives them, though we do not — which is exactly what he does say. If he had said that there *is* such a spirit, he certainly would have succeeded in denying the entailment, but he would also have suggested — in view of the concern with real existence that prompts the intermittency objection — that merely being thought of by God, mere presence in the divine understanding, is all it takes to establish the existence of an object. This, I think, he was unwilling to suggest. A similar point can be made about *Principles* 6, where Berkeley writes, 'so long as [bodies] are not actually perceived by me, or do not exist in my mind or that of any other created spirit, they must either have no existence at all, or else subsist in the mind of some eternal spirit'. Here Berkeley emphasizes the *necessity* of perception for a body's existence; he says nothing about the *sufficiency* of perception for existence — at least not in the sense of 'existence' that he so carefully delineates just a few lines before in § 3.

There is, then, no support for the perception interpretation in the passages usually claimed for it. And there is an even more serious problem: there are some passages plainly inconsistent with it.

> HYLAS: What shall we make then of the creation?
> PHILONOUS. May we not understand it to have been entirely in respect of finite spirits; so that things, with regard to us, may properly be said to begin their existence, or be created, when God decreed they should become perceptible to intelligent creatures, in that order and manner which he then established, and we now call the laws of Nature? You may call this a *relative* or *hypothetical existence* if you please. (Third Dialogue, *Works* II, p. 253)

> PHILONOUS. What would you have! do I not acknowledge a two-fold state of things, the one ectypal or natural, the other archetypal and eternal? The former was created in time; the latter existed from everlasting in the mind of God (*Works* II, p. 254)

The most important point in these passages about creation — and the one hardest to grasp, because it runs counter to our natural assumptions — is that *real* existence is *relative, hypothetical,* and *ectypal*. Existence that sounds as if it is really 'first-class' (to borrow an expression from Pitcher) — existence that is absolute, non-hypothetical, and archetypal — turns out on Berkeley's view to be insufficient for 'real' existence. These passages indicate that if we hope to understand Berkeley, we have to turn the Platonic associations of the word 'real' on their heads. 'Real' existence is not the kind of existence that every eternal entity automatically enjoys. Real existence for Berkeley is something that is entirely *relative to us*.

In the passages about creation it is God's will that is responsible for the existence of things. Far from representing a 'brief interlude' or passing flirtation, as Pitcher alleges,[29] they express a view that Berkeley affirms in an important letter to Percival, who had conveyed to Berkeley Lady Percival's concern that the immaterialism of the *Principles* might be inconsistent with the Mosaic story of creation (*Works* VIII, pp. 37-8).

The same passages about creation that rule out the perception interpretation give the phenomenalist interpretation its most convincing support. For they not only affirm that existence depends on the will of God, but assert the existence of objects when there is no human mind to perceive them. They share this second feature with the continuity argument, but that argument, unlike the passages about creation, does not ground the existence of unperceived objects in a kind of perceptibility — dependent only on the will of God — that can obtain even in the absence of finite spirits. The main obstacle to the phenomenalist interpretation has always been the large number of passages that seem to support the perception interpretation. But now that we have seen that they do not in fact support it, the way has been cleared for my own interpretation, which is basically the phenomenalist interpretation — modified, with the help of the denial of blind agency, to take account of the passages that once seemed to favor its rival.

I agree with the phenomenalist interpretation that according to Berkeley, an object exists if and only if God intends to cause certain ideas in the minds of finite spirits. Because God's intentions do not depend on the existence of finite spirits, objects can exist even if we do not. But when they do, they are not unperceived. Thanks to the denial of blind agency, God perceives every idea *by virtue of his intention to cause it*. If God did not perceive the idea, he could not intend to bring it about. Objects owe their existence to divine volitions, but those volitions cannot exist apart from the appropriate divine perceptions. The texts usually offered on behalf of the perception interpretation are therefore consistent with the phenomenalist interpretation, once it has been supplemented by the denial of blind agency. The mistake of the perception interpretation lies not in thinking that being perceived by God is necessary for the existence of an idea or object, nor even in thinking that divine perception of some sort is sufficient, but in supposing that the contribution of a perception to the reality of things is distinct from its role in constituting a volition, so that it seems as if the perception — quite apart from the volition — might support the real existence of an object on its own. On my interpretation, God certainly perceives all things, but his perception — insofar as it contributes to real existence — is nothing more than the perception inevitably involved in his volition. God's knowledge of real existence therefore derives entirely from his acquaintance with his volitions. As Malebranche says of God, 'He sees in His essence the ideas or essence of all possible beings, and in His volitions (He sees) their existence and all its circumstances'.[30] Berkeley does not share Malebranche's views on God's vision of essence, but he agrees with him, I think, that God's knowledge of real existence is acquired by attending to his will, and to his ideas only insofar as they are involved in his will.

A standard objection to including divine ideas in Berkeley's scheme of things is that they are superfluous. 'There seems', as J.D. Mabbott writes, 'to be no need whatever in such a system for the realm of God's ideas'.[31] Mabbott is right to hold that because God's ideas are, like all ideas, passive and inert, they can make no *causal* contribution to the reality of things. And if the phenomenalist interpretation is correct in claiming that Berkeley does not identify objects with ideas or collections of them, then divine ideas are not required so that we will have suitable entities with which to identify objects. But despite all this divine ideas are not, on my view, superfluous, because without them God would not only be unable to perceive, but unable to will.

Perhaps the strongest support for my interpretation is the dramatic denial of blind agency at *Philosophical commentaries* 812, already quoted above.

> The propertys of all things are in God i.e. there is in the Deity Understanding as well as Will. He is no Blind agent & in truth a blind Agent is a Contradiction.

Although this is not the only way to read the entry, it seems to me that Berkeley is deriving the conclusion that God perceives the properties of all things from the fact that he is the cause of everything. This is exactly what my interpretation requires. A similar inference may also be at work between *Commentaries* 674, where the denial of blind agency makes its first appearance in the notebooks, and 675. I quoted part of 674 above; I now quote it in its context.

> Things are two-fold active or inactive, The Existence of Active things is to act, of inactive to be perceiv'd. (entry 673)

> Distinct from or without perception there is no volition; therefore neither is their existence without perception. (entry 674)

> God May comprehend all Ideas even the Ideas wch are painfull & unpleasant without being in any degree pained thereby. Thus we our selves can imagine the pain of a burn etc without any misery or uneasiness at all. (entry 675)

The word 'their' in 674 refers back to the active things of 673. The conclusion of 674, then, is that active things cannot exist 'without perception' — that is, without perceiving, because perceiving is required for their volitional activity. In the next entry Berkeley goes on to suggest that God comprehends all things, inferring it, I think, from the conclusion of 674. Entry 675 would then say, in effect, 'God may comprehend all ideas — including pain — without thereby being pained, because he perceives pain not as its subject but as its cause'.[32]

IV. ARCHETYPES

The interpretation of unperceived objects I have proposed here helps to solve or clarify a number of difficulties in the interpretation of Berkeley. It permits, for example, a very modest construal of Berkeley's view that God's ideas are archetypes of our own. On my interpretation, to say that God's ideas are archetypes is just to say that God has ideas of the ideas he causes in us, or (taking into account the relaxed attitude towards sameness expressed in the Third Dialogue) that God has the *same* ideas he causes in us. Because God is the cause, it is appropriate to speak of his ideas as patterns, originals, or archetypes. There is, then, no need to be troubled by the relationship between our ideas and God's. If we understand the relation between cause and effect, as well as the relation of idea to action in a spiritual cause, there is nothing more to the relation of idea to archetype that remains to be understood.

Berkeley is presumably committed to the view that God's ideas are in some way resemblances of ours (how else could they be ideas 'of' ours?; see also *Principles* 90), but this should occasion no difficulty. Any difficulty it does occasion can be put down to the limitations of a finite mind. In view of the inescapability of the conclusion that ideas of sense have a spiritual cause who knows and comprehends all things, it would be rash to respond in any other way. To borrow a passage from Locke: 'God is a simple being, omniscient, that knows all things possible; and omnipotent, that can do or make all things possible. But how he knows, or how he makes, I do not conceive: his ways of knowing as well as his ways of creating, are to me incomprehensible'.[33]

This is a modest view of the archetypes. But it accords with Berkeley's reluctance to endorse the more elaborate proposals put forward by Johnson (see *Works* II, pp. 274-6 and 285-6 for Johnson, and p. 292 for Berkeley), and there is no text that calls for a bolder interpretation. This is true even of *Siris*, whose divine ideas, in the opinion of some, are the archetypes of the *Dialogues* Platonized. The relevant passages in *Siris* have nothing to do with archetypes of corporeal objects; when Berkeley speaks of entities 'distinct or separate from all sensible and corporeal beings' (§323) he is thinking not of archetypes but spirits. The divine ideas of *Siris* are neither the abstract ideas of the *Principles* nor the archetypes of the *Dialogues;* they are notions, or aspects of notions.[34]

V.   CONCLUSION

In his second contribution to his correspondence with Clarke, Leibniz writes that 'the reason why God perceives every thing, is not his bare presence, but also his operation. 'Tis because he preserves things by an action, which continually produces whatever is good and perfect in them' (p. 17).[35] Leibniz repeats the point several times (see for example pp. 41 and 83), and some of his statements could be inserted into Berkeley's *Principles* without disturbing the flow of the argument:

> He perceives them, because they proceed from him; if one may be allowed to say, that he *perceives* them: which ought not to be said, unless we divest that word of its imperfection; for else it seems to signify, that things act upon him. They exist, and are known to him, because he understands and wills them; and because what he wills, is the same as what exists. (p. 84)

Unperceived objects and Berkeley's denial of blind agency

Clarke's response is that the belief 'God perceives and knows all things, not by being present to them, but by continually producing them anew; is a mere fiction of the schoolmen, without any proof' (p. 109). No doubt Leibniz was aware of the scholastic precedent, but he approved of the view because it served to unite two great truths: the first that God perceives the actual in a way he does not perceive the merely possible; the second that existing things owe their existence to God's will. In this paper I have tried to show how the denial of blind agency allows Berkeley to combine the same two truths. If we accept the perception interpretation we cannot say that what actually exists depends on the will of God; this brings us up against Berkeley's insistence that it does. If we accept the unmodified phenomenalist interpretation we have no reason to say that God's perception of the actual differs from his perception of the merely possible; this brings us up against the criticisms so forcefully expressed by Pitcher. The interpretation I have provided offers a way out.[36]

Notes

1. E. M. Forster. *The longest journey* (New York, 1962), p. 2.
2. Forster, p. 1.
3. Forster, pp. 1-2.
4. Sources of quotations from Berkeley are cited in the text. I quote from A. A. Luce and T.E. Jessop (eds.), *The works of George Berkeley. Bishop of Cloyne* (London, 1948-57).
5. *Berkeley* (London, 1977), p. 175.
6. Pitcher makes this point himself on pp. 178-9. There are times, however, when Berkeley uses the word 'perception' to *exclude* non-sensory perception. See for example *Philosophical commentaries* 582.
7. I believe the expression 'theocentric phenomenalism' was first used in connection with Berkeley by J.O. Wisdom, *The unconscious origin of Berkeley's philosophy* (London, 1953), p. 21.
8. For such a verdict see John Stuart Mill. 'Berkeley's life and writings', in the *Collected works of John Stuart Mill*. vol. 11 (Toronto, 1978), pp. 460-1, and Pitcher. pp. 166-7, 171.
9. *The philosophical writings of Descartes*, translated by John Cottingham. Robert Stoothoff, and Dugald Murdoch (Cambridge, 1984-5), vol. 2, p. 26.
10. *Philosophical letters*, translated by Anthony Kenny (Oxford, 1970), p. 102. The following quotation comes from p. 118. Both letters were published in the 17th century.
11. *The search after truth*, 3.1.1, section 1. I quote from the translation by Thomas M. Lennon and Paul J. Olscamp (Columbus, Ohio, 1980), p. 199.
12. *Search after truth*. 3.2.3, pp. 223-4 in Lennon and Olscamp.
13. *Search after truth*. 3.2.6, p. 230 in Lennon and Olscamp.
14. *The correspondence of John Locke*. vol, 7, edited by E. S. DeBeer (Oxford, 1982) p. 408. I quote from the editor's translation of the Latin original.
15. *Correspondence*. pp. 411, 410. The denial of blind agency is also prominent in the *Essay* (see for example II xxi 6-10) and in §1 of *Of the conduct of the understanding*.
16. For an interpretation of Berkeley that lends proper emphasis to the intimate connection

99

Kenneth P. Winkler

between understanding and will see M. R. Ayers's introduction to his edition of George Berkeley, *Philosophical Works* (London, 1975), especially p. xvi.

17. For King, whose discussion of this issue was strongly influenced by Locke, see *An essay on the origin of evil* (a translation of *de origine mali*, originally published in 1702) (London, 1731), 1.3.8 and II.1.2.2; for Sergeant, *Solid philosophy asserted* (London, 1697), pp. 219, 225; for Norris, *The theory and regulation of love* (Oxford, 1688), Appendix. It might be objected that blind agency was allowed by philosophers and theologians who denied that the will always follows the last judgment of the understanding. But even 'voluntarists' who denied the *primacy* of the understanding shared Locke's assumption that the understanding, viewed as a faculty of simple apprehension, provides the will with its content or specification. For an illustration of this point in a 17th-century context see Norman L. Fiering, *Moral philosophy at seventeenth century Harvard* (Chapel Hill, 1981), pp. 104-46.

18. Aside from the passages I go on to discuss see *Works* II, p. 220 (in the Second Dialogue) and pp. 236-9 (in the Third Dialogue). The second passage should be read along with *Commentaries* 177a and 780.

19. Jonathan Bennett, *Locke, Berkeley, Hume: central themes* (Oxford, 1971), p. 168.

20. Bennett, pp. 170-1. Pitcher agrees with Bennett that Berkeley's argument conflates 'two quite distinct conceptions of an idea' *depending on* a mind' (p. 177). Bennett's accusation is also endorsed by Ian Tipton, *Berkeley: The philosophy of immaterialism* (London, 1974), pp. 323, 383-4.

21. Bennett, pp. 170-1.

22. Bennett, p. 165. For his reconstruction of the continuity argument see p. 169.

23. Bennett, p. 185.

24. Bennett, p. 168, note 9.

25. This point was brought home to me at the Dublin conference by Tim Williamson.

26. Pitcher, pp. 171-2.

27. Pitcher, p. 171.

28. The passages, arranged in three groups, are presented on pp. 175-8.

29. Pitcher, p. 172.

30. *Search after truth* 4.11.3, p. 319 in Lennon and Olscamp.

31. J. D. Mabbott, 'The place of God in Berkeley's philosophy', reprinted in David M. Armstrong and C. B. Martin (eds.), *Locke and Berkeley* (Garden City, N.Y., 1968), p. 369. I too have suggested (mistakenly, I now believe) that God's ideas are superfluous. See the introduction to my edition of Berkeley's *A treatise concerning the principles of human knowledge* (Indianapolis, 1982), pp. xxxii-iii.

32. For interpretations similar to the one proposed in this section but differently developed see Charles J. McCracken, 'What *does* Berkeley's God see in the quad?', *Archiv für Geschichte der Philosophie* 61 (1979), pp. 280-92, especially pp. 288-90, and Noel Fleming, 'The tree in the quad', *American Philosophical Quarterly* 22 (1985), pp. 25-36. Ian Tipton anticipates all three interpretations in note 12 on p. 385 of *Berkeley: the philosophy of immaterialism*.

33. *An examination of P. Malebranche's opinion*, in *The works of John Locke* (London, 1823), vol. 9, p. 255.

34. My interpretation of *Siris* cannot be fully documented here but the relevant sections are 306-8, 330, 335-6, and 350.

35. All page references in this paragraph are to H. A. Alexander's edition of *The Leibniz-Clarke correspondence* (Manchester, 1956).

36. I have received helpful suggestions from many people. I am especially grateful to Margaret Atherton, Charles McCracken, Robert McKim, and Margaret Wilson, all of whom provided written comments.

Ireland and the critique
of mercantilism in Berkeley's
Querist

by Patrick Kelly

Although it has long been recognized that Berkeley's *Querist* sprang from an 'urgent, pressing problem of unemployment and poverty', the occasion of the three hundredth anniversary of his birth seems a fitting point to consider in what precise way experience of Irish conditions influenced Berkeley's economic thinking.[1] Can it be argued that circumstances in early eighteenth-century Ireland provided a privileged perspective that enabled the philosopher bishop to repudiate the Midas fixation of earlier British writers and to break with the identification of money with gold and silver, conceiving it instead as a 'ticket or counter' — the two major achievements with which historians of economics traditionally credit him?[2] In seeking to answer this question I shall consider Berkeley's ideas both in relation to conditions in Ireland and in the context of a specifically Irish literature in which the problems of the Irish economy had since the pioneering writings of Sir William Petty in the later seventeenth century been seen as a special case requiring rather different solutions from those of the prosperous economies of England, Holland, and France. This Irish tradition within British mercantilist writing may be compared with a rather similar Scots tradition, whose foremost exponent John Law has often been taken as Berkeley's immediate forerunner in the field of monetary theory.[3]

Before embarking on the exploration of the context of Berkeley's economic thinking something must be said about the texts, namely *The querist, containing several queries proposed to the consideration of the public* (1735-7) and the two other main pieces of economic interest in the Berkeley canon, *An essay towards preventing the ruin of Great Britain* (1721) and *A word to the wise, or an exhortation to the Roman Catholic clergy of Ireland* (1749). *The querist* is unusual, though by no means unique in the early literature of political economy, in consisting of a series of randomly linked questions, largely (though not entirely) of an economic import, which number just short of nine hundred, and were issued in three parts in the years 1735, 1736, and 1737. The first edition was anonymous, and it was not till 1750 that a second bearing Berkeley's name (but omitting 345 of the original queries and including 45 fresh ones) appeared.[4] The format and a certain tendency to repetitiveness make it difficult to follow the precise thread of Berkeley's ideas on certain issues, even in comparison with the often haphazard nature of economic writing generally before the mid-eighteenth century. Berkeley's earlier piece, the *Essay towards preventing the ruin of Great Britain*, had been addressed to the British public on the occasion of the collapse of the South Sea Bubble, and, while containing various ideas about the nature of wealth to be found in the two later works, is notable for the moral dimension which it injects into economic discourse. Honest provision for a reasonable livelihood through labour and frugality is urged in place of frenzied speculation, while luxury and extravagance are shown to be the path to moral, political, and economic ruin for nations as well as individuals. The third work, *A word to the wise*, is informed by the same public-spirited concern for the common good and conviction of the moral and spiritual worth of honest labour. In it Berkeley addresses himself to the Catholic clergy, calling on them to promote the material welfare of their flocks by dissuading their parishioners from idleness and beggary.

From these writings Berkeley emerges as one familiar with the economic thought of his age, even though specific references to other works are rare indeed. To speak of economic thought in the context of the first half of the eighteenth century is, however, to introduce an anachronism. Although 'Trade' was reasonably clearly delineated as a field of inquiry by 1720, it was by no means as yet seen as an autonomous subject, and its relations with other branches of what would now be considered as economics, such as coinage and revenue, were far from clear.[5] Economics remained very much a subordinate field of politics and administration, though one increasingly recognized as of major importance. Amongst the accepted principles of early eighteenth-century thought was the recognition that wealth was the creation of human labour, that provision of suitable employment was a major goal of state policy, and that an adequate volume of the circulating medium was essential to sustain economic activity. The earlier preoccupation with the achievement of a favourable trade balance in terms of specie was beginning to yield place to concern over the labour implications of exports and imports, and commerce both domestic and even foreign was coming to be seen as a mutually beneficial exchange of surplus products. The quarter century of peace in Europe following the Treaty of Utrecht (1713) and the re-expansion of world trade were rendering obsolete earlier mercantilist notions of a strictly limited volume of

Ireland and the critique of mercantilism in Berkeley's *Querist*

international trade in which one nation could only benefit at another's loss. Much of Europe in the 1720s stood on the threshold of prosperity, and though economic thinking generally lagged behind economic developments a sense of optimism can be discerned in English and French writings from the later 1720s. Such, however, was not the case in Ireland, where conditions in the 1720s and early 1730s remained extremely depressed, and writers became increasingly convinced that they were confronted by problems peculiar to the Irish situation, which taken together (for parallels could be found for particular difficulties in other countries) made Ireland a unique case requiring special solutions.

The idea that the Irish economy constituted a special case because of its relative backwardness and political dependence can be traced back to William Petty's *Treatise of taxes and contributions* (1662), and was clearly articulated in two further works which he wrote in the 1670s, *The political anatomy of Ireland* and *Political arithmetic*, published in 1691 and 1690 respectively. In these works Petty distinguished between what he termed 'local' (or 'domestick') and 'universal' wealth; the first being food, clothing, houses, agricultural improvements, fortifications, roads, navigation works, and industrial buildings and equipment, and the second the gold and silver which a nation obtained through international trade. Though nations should chiefly pursue the latter 'which are not perishable, nor so mutable as other Commodities, but are Wealth at all times, and [in] all places', Petty also suggested that a poor nation such as Ireland might do better in the short-term to concentrate on the production of 'local' wealth to provide the necessary base from which to expand into the competitive world of international trade.[6] It was this perception of the implications of the distinction between a dependent and backward economy and those of England and Holland, where a substantial part of the population were already largely dependent on production for international trade that was the foundation of the Irish tradition in economic writing. The other features which Petty saw as distinguishing Ireland were relative underpopulation, putting the ratio of people to land at one tenth of that of England, and one hundredth of that of Holland (with all the diseconomy of scale this would impose for military, administrative, ecclesiastical, and commercial purposes), and the existence of a large section of the population cut off from the monetary economy, who lacked the appetite for consumption that would stir them to produce for the market. More sympathetic to the predicament of the Irish poor than many later writers (including Berkeley), Petty did not attribute this disinclination to labour to any innate moral or physical characteristics, blaming instead the ease with which life could be sustained at a basic level of subsistence in Ireland, the lack of economic incentives, and their recent treatment by the English. Other significant differences from England included the appalling currency provisions, 'the Difference, Confusion and Badness of the Moneys', and the distorting impact on the balance of payments arising from the remittance of rents to absentees.[7]

The continuity between the problems which Petty identified as peculiar to the Irish economy and those which faced Berkeley and his contemporaries was, according to the most recent historian of the Irish economy in the eighteenth century, perhaps more apparent to the thinkers of the time than is altogether justifiable in reality.[8] While the eighteenth-century writers considered ostensibly very similar problems, they did so in the course of a period of acute and prolonged decline. Petty was aware that despite the difficulties which he highlighted, conditions for even the poorest in Ireland had improved in the twenty years since the Rebellion and Civil Wars (1641-52) and a note of optimism lies behind his diagnosis of the country's ills. By the later 1720s, while the hope of achieving prosperity in the long run still remained, it was very much compromised by the conviction that commercial jealousy in England would endanger any success in Ireland. As Archbishop King perceived even before the beginning of the eighteenth century, English resentment was directed not at particular industries in Ireland but at the very notion of prosperity in the colony.[9] From the single instance of prohibiting live cattle exports in Petty's time English intervention at Ireland's expense had extended to more rigorous enforcement of the Navigation Laws, to a further civil war in 1689-91 followed by land confiscations and a settlement (itself reversed by an English act of resumption in 1700), and above all to the prohibition on the export of woollen cloth imposed by the English parliament in 1699. The sense of frustration and despair at English inability or unwillingness to cope with Irish problems reached a peak in the Bank Controversy of 1720-1 and the Wood's Halfpence affair of 1723-5.[10]

As far back as the woollen export controversy of the 1690s this feeling had received overt political expression in William Molyneux's *Case of Ireland stated* (1698), which argued on the basis of natural right that Irishmen should direct their own affairs. In the intervening period a sense of colonial nationhood had begun to emerge with a consciousness of being Irishmen, as opposed to

104

Ireland and the critique of mercantilism in Berkeley's *Querist*

merely Englishmen living in Ireland, and a corresponding sense of patriotism had become widespread amongst the Anglo-Irish élite, amongst the professional and commercial middle classes, and, particularly in the capital, even amongst the protestant people and artizans. This nascent sense of Irish nationalism had been fuelled by Swift's *Drapier's letters* and other successful manifestations of resistance which had forced withdrawal of Wood's copper coinage patent by the Walpole government in 1725. But the economic problems, particularly the grossly ill-functioning currency system which Wood's coin had ostensibly been intended to ameliorate, had not been overcome. With a continuing down-swing in agriculture from 1726 leading to famine conditions in 1728-9, and growing difficulties in international trade, a fresh wave of economic literature started appearing in 1728 which may be regarded as the immediate background to *The querist*.[11]

The most distinguished of these economic pamphlets of the late 1720s and early 1730s was the *List of absentees* detailing the burden on the Irish economy of payments to absentee landlords, office-holders, and beneficiaries under family settlements, written by Berkeley's friend Thomas Prior. But its impact has since been overshadowed by Swift's famous *Modest proposal* in which the genre of economic projecting (in the eighteenth-century sense, not the twentieth) was ironically exploited in a savage attack on the country's inability to provide for the mass of its population. Another notable work was Arthur Dobbs's *Essay on the trade and improvement of Ireland*, published in two parts in 1729 and 1731. Dobbs, an associate of Prior in the founding of the Dublin Society and a future Governor of North Carolina, analysed the statistics of Ireland's foreign trade and subsequently her internal problems. Several pamphlets were specifically directed at the currency difficulties. James Maculla, the original opponent of Wood's project, again initiated the debate by calling for an issue of copper to supply the need for small change. Others advocated a revaluation of the gold and silver moneys to combat the predominance of Portuguese moidores (gold pieces passing at an excessive rate of £1-10s-0d), whose low rate of circulation was a further clog on trade.[12] Prior also participated in the currency discussions in another well-known work, entitled *Observations of coin in general* (1729), in which the dominant influence of Locke's pamphlets on Irish monetary writing is particularly visible. Two works from the pen of the unjustly neglected David Bindon also dealt with currency questions in 1729; the second of which, *A scheme for supplying industrious men with money to carry on their trades, and for better providing for the poor of Ireland,* proposed creating Lombards, or *monti di pietá* on the Italian model, in every city and town in Ireland to supply capital for enterprising, small tradesmen. In 1730-1 the debate extended to take in the woollen question and press the British for concessions on this front; amongst the participants were again David Bindon and Sir John Browne who had earlier written on trade and currency, and a newcomer in the person of Lord Percival, son of Berkeley's long-time correspondent. Archbishop Synge initiated proposals for charity schools, and attention was also given to the question of the public debt and the possibility of reducing the legal rate of interest (brought down to 6% in 1732).

The two main problems which Berkeley confronts in *The querist,* namely employment and currency, thus constituted the major practical concerns of immediately contemporary writings in Ireland. It is also clear that he shared with these contemporaries a common theoretical assumption which served as the basis of their analysis in terms of what Marian Bowley has called the 'necessary stock of money' approach.[13] The idea is succinctly expressed by Prior at the start of the Observations, which conclude the *List of absentees:*

> Money being the Measure of all Commerce, a certain Quantity thereof is necessary, for the carrying on the Trade of each Country, in Proportion to the Business thereof.[14]

The origin of this concept is to be found in Petty, who compared money to 'the Fat of the Body-politick, whereof too much doth often hinder its Agility, as too little of it makes it sick . . . '.[15] It was amplified by Locke who traced the requirements for money in the economy by examining the size of the transaction balances needed by the different sectors, such as landlords and tenants, employers and workmen, &c.[16] The notion was further developed in the 1690s by Charles Davenant, a writer much drawn on by Irish economic thinkers of Berkeley's day, who restated the concept in dynamic terms thereby emphasizing the unique potential for economic stimulus afforded by a growing circulation of money.[17] By the 1720s and 1730s the concept of the capacity of an expanding circulation to break through stagnation and overcome the underemployment of resources both human and material, already very much implicit in Locke's analysis, had become the accepted orthodoxy. Thomas Prior argued that Ireland's relative prosperity following the Jacobite War which culminated in the boom in woollen exports of the late 1690s had been a direct consequence of the influx of money occasioned by English and French expenditure on the war. But 'of late, that Treasure, which was the Fruit and Acquisition of many Years, hath gradually flow'd from us', with the result that interest rates had risen because of the scarcity of money.

> This Want of Money in the Kingdom throws a Damp upon all Business; Manufacturers can't be set to work, Materials purchas'd, or Credit subsist; and People, who are willing to support themselves by their Industry, are left to struggle with Poverty, for Want of Employment.[18]

For Dobbs scarcity of money had deprived farmers of a market for their produce so that they were unable to pay their rents or continue to employ their labourers; foreign merchants took advantage of the lack of money to force down the price of manufactures, and the consequences were nationwide idleness and vagrancy.[19]

The call to increase the volume of monetary circulation in practice covered two demands which, with the growth of credit arrangements, were now coming to be understood as distinct phenomena in a way that had not been so readily apparent in the seventeenth century. The first was the shortage of capital for productive activity, particularly for the small artisan and tradesman, and the second was the physical shortage of coin to service transactions and the impact which this had on price levels. That Ireland was short of coin in the 1720s and 1730s seems beyond question. No Irish silver money had been coined since the reign of James I in 1605 and though a small amount of copper halfpence and farthings had been issued in the later seventeenth century, the economy was largely dependent on English money and a wide variety of Continental coins, often of inferior quality. In order to keep such a currency system functioning even reasonably effectively, correct ratios had to be maintained between gold and silver, and between the precious metals and their nominal rating in pounds Irish.

The period from Charles II to William III saw several alterations in the Irish standard, of which the most successful in attracting coin into the country was the high valuation of 1695. In 1701, however, the nominal value of both gold and silver was reduced to levels that remained constant till the separate Irish pound disappeared in 1826. In the later 1720s the Irish ratio was particularly unfavourable in international terms and led to an outflow of both precious metals, though silver was worse affected than gold.[20] It was this state of affairs that accounted for the concern of Prior, Bindon, and others to have the Irish currency rerated in order to attract back silver into the country and also to have a copper issue to provide small change. In arguing for a paper currency to supplement the circulation of gold and silver Berkeley was almost unique amongst the Irish writers of his day.[21] The attitude of the other participants in the debate was characterized by Prior, who viewed the issue of paper currency with horror. Like earlier English and Scots opponents of paper-money, Prior believed that the inevitable consequence would be a rapid collapse in the exchange value of the paper-money and the draining of the country of its remaining gold and silver — both of which Prior claimed had been the experience of the paper issues of the British colonies in North America.[22]

That Berkeley should, virtually alone, have advocated the issue of paper-money in Ireland might well appear to be a consequence of his first-hand experience of American conditions, the one respect in which he differed so notably from contemporary Irish writers. While it was true that some colonial issues in the early eighteenth century had led to the problems to which Prior adverted, others had been extremely successful and had revived the declining economies of Delaware, Pennsylvania, and New Jersey.[23] Yet though Rhode Island itself had successfully pioneered a paper-money issue backed by the mortgaging of land, the American experience does not seem to have lain directly behind Berkeley's proposals in *The querist*. The various references to paper issues in America are less than enthusiastic about their practical success, though difficulties are attributed to faults in management rather than to the inherent shortcomings of paper-money as such.[24] Queries 251-2 instance some unnamed American towns as evidence of the feasibility of sustaining all the requirements of civil life, 'although there be not one grain of gold and silver current among them'. There is no reason to believe that Berkeley was familiar with the growing American literature on paper-money, though 1729, the year he landed in Rhode Island, saw the appearance of Benjamin Franklin's *Modest enquiry into the nature and necessity of a paper currency*, a work which bears comparison with the best European writing on the subject by this date.[25]

On the contrary the path along which Berkeley seems to have been led to his radical conclusions about the nature of money and wealth would seem to have its origins firmly rooted in his analysis of Ireland's current difficulties. The key to the arguments of *The querist* lies in Berkeley's rejection of the chief bastion of mercantilist thinking, namely that national wealth is universally dependent on foreign trade. This argument had been regarded as axiomatic since the debate between Malynes, Misselden and Mun in the early 1620s and had received its classic formulation in the latter's *England's treasure by forraign trade* (1664).[26] For Berkeley this maxim notoriously failed to hold good in the case of Ireland; as Q. 325 asks: 'Whether there may not be found a people who so contrive to be impoverished by their [foreign] trade? And whether we are not that people?' As Swift had already implicitly suggested in *A short view of the state of Ireland* (1728), Berkeley argued that for a poor agricultural economy such as Ireland to export the resources so desperately needed to sustain its own unemployed masses in exchange for luxury imports to gratify the vanity of the landowning gentry was not the way to wealth but to destruction (QQ. 169, 173). As Q. 175 figuratively expressed it: 'Whether she would not be a very vile matron, and justly thought either mad or foolish, that should give away the necessaries of life from her naked and famished children, in exchange for pearls to stick in her hair, and sweetmeats to please her own palate?' Unlike Swift, Berkeley was able to build on this perception and propose an alternative in the form of a largely self-sufficient economy in which the provision for mutual needs, given a realization of their true interest by the Irish gentry, would create a self-sustaining prosperity, made possible by a state-issued paper currency backed by land (QQ. 127, 217).

Since such a reading of *The querist* challenges accepted views, this claim obviously requires further substantiation. Despite the generally rather confused presentation of the argument in *The querist*, the main points of the argument which Berkeley builds on his rejection of foreign trade as the way to wealth are clearly discernable in the first forty queries, and can be summed up as follows:

(1) The wealth of a nation consists in the proper feeding, clothing, and housing of the mass of the population.
(2) This wealth is created by human industry.
(3) The aim of the state should therefore be to encourage the industry of its inhabitants.
(4) Money is only useful insofar as it serves to stimulate industry.
(5) Money is only valuable insofar as it represents power over the products of the industry of others.
(6) Power relates to appetite, which in turn is largely dependent on fashion.
(7) The state should seek to control fashion, and thus direct the appetite of the people.

Patrick Kelly

(8) The gentry [presumably as the consumption class] set the pattern of aspirations for the rest of the people.
(9) Successful regulation of the economy so as to achieve (1) depends on educating the gentry as to their real interest.
(10) The Irish are prevented from 'thriving by that cynical content in dirt...[exceeding] any other people in Christendom'.
(11) The Irish can only be made industrious by awakening in them an appetite for a reasonable standard of living.
(12) Given basic geographic and climatic factors, a country's wealth is proportionate to the industry of its people, which in turn depends on 'the circulation of credit, be the credit circulated or transferred by what marks so ever'.
(13) 'The true idea of money as such . . . [is] that of a ticket or counter.'
(14) Since the attainment of (1) depends on the will or opinion of the people, this may be achieved without the mediation of gold and silver in exchange.

These propositions make clear that for Berkeley successful management of the economy depends on understanding the relationship between the true idea of wealth and the true idea of money (Q. 114). As Q. 48 puts it: 'Whether our real defect [in economic policy] be not a wrong way of thinking?' The 'universal' wealth that gold and silver constituted for Petty and Locke is for Berkeley a general idea without a corresponding reality; for him there can be 'no greater mistake in politics than to measure the wealth of a nation by its gold and silver' (Q 465). Furnished with a true understanding of wealth, it becomes possible to establish the goal of national policy, namely the well-being of the whole population through full employment (QQ. 131, 329, 345). The achievement of this is the duty of the legislature, and great care must therefore be given to the proper education of its members (QQ. 183, 193, 195). In determining what must be done, the resources of statistical knowledge (political arithmetic) must be used to discover the exact condition of the nation (QQ. 495, 530). The original definition of wealth is reiterated and amplified on several occasions; the 'plenty of all the necessaries and comforts of life' of Q. 542 is shown to be a limited objective, quite different from the endless accumulation of gold and silver. Queries 304 and 306 suggest that natural appetites like natural powers are limited, and that to attempt to provide for more than this is a delusion of fancy that leads men 'into endless pursuits and wild labyrinths'.

Given an understanding of the possibility of providing for the mutual needs of the population without reliance on foreign trade, simply by applying the industry of the population to the natural resources of the country, the problem remains how to motivate the mass of the population to labour for their own advantage. For Berkeley the solution is partly psychological and partly technical, i.e. how to transform wants and needs into effective demand in economic terms. Not only are the Irish the 'most indolent and supine people in Christendom' (Q. 357) thanks to their mixed Spanish and Tartar descent (QQ. 513-4), but they suffer from a degree of misery and despair that inhibit their taking to productive activity; 'nastiness and beggary . . . extinguish all such ambition [for prosperity], making men listless, hopeless and slothful'.[28] The solution is to motivate them by giving them a taste of prosperity and letting them share in the wealth which they create. Once they are used to eating beef and wearing shoes, they will seek to improve their condition still further and labour to create wealth (QQ. 20, 353, 355). If a taste for prosperity failed to awaken an inclination to labour, Berkeley saw the state as justified in using force to compel the idle to work (QQ. 383-6). Industry was a 'habit which like other habits may by time and skill be introduced among any people', and children in particular should be inured to it early (QQ. 378, 371). Establishment of prosperity was seen by Berkeley as a self-fuelling activity, a higher standard of living would increase the population (without Malthusian consequences), and this in time would provide a surplus over and above immediate requirements that would make possible a limited and strictly controlled foreign trade (QQ. 107, 128); but of this more will be said later.

The other problem in the creation of the self-sufficient economy was the translation of the mutual needs of the population into effective demand in economic terms, and this brings us to the consideration of Berkeley's theory of money. In the past Berkeley has been seen as simply applying to the solution of Ireland's difficulties a theory of paper-money already formulated from his reading of Law's *Money and trade considered* (1705) and his knowledge of banking and credit elsewhere in the world.[29] Such a view can be challenged, however, by showing how Berkeley's ideas on paper-money logically derive from his analysis of Ireland's difficulties that resulted in his definition of real wealth. He starts by examining the value and utility of money in the conventional form of gold and silver. Its value is the power which it confers over the product of the labour of others and its utility is in 'stirr[ing] up industry, [and] enabling men to participate [in] the fruits of each other's industry' (Q.5). This prompts two questions: 'Whether any other means, equally conducing to excite and circulate the industry of mankind, may not be useful as money?', and 'Whether he who could have everthing else at his wish or will would value money?' (QQ. 6, 7). Q. 8 then brings in the role of the state by proposing that the objective of the well-governed state would be to ensure that 'each member, according to his just pretensions and industry, should have power'. Here then the theoretical basis of the argument is complete: by creating paper-money the state transforms the needs and wants of individuals into effective demand proportionate to their labour product, which provides the stimulus of credit necessary to marry wants and industry within the closed economy.

Although the definition of money in *The querist* that has most caught the attention of commentators is that in Q. 23: 'Whether the true idea of money, as such, be not altogether that of a ticket or counter', Berkeley's main emphasis is not on the inert function of the medium of exchange but rather the credit creating role of the circulating medium, the 'ticket entitling to power' of Q. 441. Since coin and paper-money are seen as tokens of the power over goods and services represented by money (Q. 475), the actual material of which the ticket is constituted is not of particular consequence. Indeed QQ. 226 and 445 suggest that paper may serve the function of money more effectively than gold or silver. Such a view depends largely on a quantity theorem approach to the exchange value of money, such as had earlier been propounded by Locke; as Q. 465 expresses it: 'Whether *ceteris paribus*, it be not true that the prices of things increase as the quantity of money increaseth, and are diminished as it is diminished?', and Q. 310 further makes clear how the value of the counters is determined by their total quantity in relation to the goods on offer for them.[30] But in considering the issue of paper-money by a national bank Berkeley is not content to allow its value to be determined simply by the operations of the quantity theorem, but assumes that it must also be backed by the credit of land, thereby seeking to provide this paper-money with an intrinsic value analogous to the intrinsic value of gold and silver money. And it is this inability to conceive of a true paper currency even within the closed economy that perhaps explains the great Joseph Schumpeter's otherwise puzzling characterization of Berkeley as a concealed metallist.[31] Berkeley is well aware that with a money whose value is determined both by the quantity theorem and by a backing there will be problems of management, but considers that these can relatively easily be overcome by 'a little sense and honesty', (Q.247). Only a national bank with the public as its stock-holder can fulfil this role (Om. Q. I, 222); to allow a private individual to 'create a hundred pounds with a stroke of his pen' (Q. 290) is to give him too great an advantage, and further risks the "Wealth and prosperity" of the country on the honesty of a single Banker' (Q. 275). Such individuals are further tempted to endanger the currency by stock-jobbing for their private advantage (QQ. 308, 429). A public bank brings the stock and credit of the nation to back its currency (Q. 277). But Berkeley also concedes that the management of a land-backed currency will be complicated by the way in which land values may be expected to rise as a result of the additional utility such an institution will confer on land, and claims that the defect of Law's proposed bank in Scotland lay in insufficient control over the issue of notes, because of landowners' overeagerness to mortgage the full value of their estates.[32] Unfortunately the method of the presentation of Berkeley's ideas in *The querist* makes it difficult to work out the full implications of his proposals for the backing of paper-money. Indeed in this respect the format of *The querist* allowed him to raise suggestions that seem logically incompatible, and one can well understand Schumpeter's despairing conclusion (largely in relation to Berkeley) that 'views on money are as difficult to describe as are shifting clouds'.[33] Even the notion of money as 'a ticket or counter' when examined in detail is by no means the startling advance on Locke's monetary theory which it appears to be at first. In his explication of the quantity theorem Locke had argued that given an island cut off from commerce with the rest of the world, the value of its currency would be determined by the quantity of commodities on offer, and the substance of the money would be immaterial so long as it could not be arbitrarily increased in quantity, and there was sufficient to serve the transaction needs of the community. While Locke, however, concluded that such conditions were not likely to occur in reality,[34] Berkeley by rejecting the utility of foreign trade in Ireland's case was able to apply this insight to the solution of the problem of creating effective demand in the closed economy. But in seeking to explain why people should be prepared to accept money in exchange for commodities Berkeley, like Locke, was driven back on the idea of the need for some form of intrinsic value, namely the backing of his paper-money by land.[35]

This conclusion to our examination of Berkeley's theory of money emphasizes his debt like that of the generality of his Irish contemporaries to Locke's writings on money (though not, it must be stressed, the material on money in *Two treatises*). And in relating Berkeley to Locke, whose concept of money was so heavily influenced by his

Patrick Kelly

belief in the primacy of foreign as opposed to domestic trade, it is necessary to say a further word about Berkeley's ideas on foreign trade. Although Berkeley considered that real wealth could be achieved by a nation without resort to foreign trade, he was in the end reluctantly led to permit some degree of foreign trade. He seems to suggest that even in the short term if luxury items were excluded, a small volume of foreign trade could be sustained without damage to the country (Q. 170). But in the long term the prosperity created by a flourishing domestic trade would 'produce numbers and industry, the consequence whereof would be foreign trade and riches, *how unnecessary soever*' (Q. 128, my italics). The implication of this process is, however, very significant; what Berkeley means is that by this stage Ireland would have ceased to be a poor country and might thus participate in international trade on a par with rich countries like Holland and England. Even this foreign trade would, however, need to be strictly controlled (Q. 554), and would be an exchange of foreign commodities for 'domestic superfluities' (Q. 172).

Berkeley should therefore rightly be considered not so much as one who completely rejected mercantilist theory in its mature form as evolved in Britain in the later seventeenth and early eighteenth centuries but as an early proponent of the distinction between the economies of rich and poor countries that would so exercise the attention of Hume, Smith, Steuart, and other writers of the third quarter of the eighteenth century.[36] For all his repudiation of the axiom that foreign trade was the key to wealth, Berkeley remained firmly entrenched in the mercantilist tradition in many important respects. The extraordinary degree of control which he was prepared to accord to the state reveals his firm commitment to the household model of the economy and measures how far his approach was from any form of economic liberalism. It was Irish circumstances that opened his eyes to the illusion that gold and silver represented wealth and also led him to seek a substitute for the circulation of gold and silver moneys to stimulate the economy. From the extremely conventional approach at a theoretical level taken in his early *Essay towards preventing the ruin of Great Britain* there is nothing to suggest that had he not been led to turn his attention to the special circumstances of the Irish economy, he would otherwise have reached a more innovative position. As it was, by doing so he reversed the distinction drawn by Petty in *Political anatomy* and demonstrated that 'local' wealth was indeed real and 'universal'.

114

Ireland and the critique of mercantilism in Berkeley's *Querist*

Notes

1. Douglas Vickers, *Studies in the theory of money, 1690-1776* (1960), p. 145.
2. E.g., R.H.I. Palgrave, ed., *Dictionary of Political Economy* (3rd edn., 3 vols., 1925-6), s.v.
3. Vickers, op. cit., p. 141. For an illuminating discussion of the Scots literature, see J. M. Low, 'A regional example of mercantilist theory', *Manchester School of Economic and Social Studies*, 21 (1953), 62-84.
4. Citations from *The querist* are from the edn. printed in Joseph Johnston. *Bishop Berkeley's* Querist *in historical perspective* (Dundalk, 1970), based on the text of the 1752 edn. as modified in *The works of George Berkeley*, vol. VI, ed. T. E. Jessop (1953); this gives the 595 Queries of the 1750 edn. followed by the omitted Queries. divided into three sections corresponding to original three parts of the book. References are to Q., or Om. Q., respectively. For full bibliographical details of the three works mentioned, see Geoffrey Keynes, *A bibliography of George Berkeley, Bishop of Cloyne* (Oxford, 1976).
5. Cf. William Letwin, *The origins of scientific economics* (1963), pp. 214-18.
6. *The economic writings of Sir William Petty*, ed. C.H. Hull (2 vols., 1963 reprint), I, 147, 256-7, 295.
7. Ibid, I, 183-202.
8. L.M. Cullen, *An economic history of Ireland since 1660* (1972), pp. 39-49; and 'Landlords, bankers and merchants: the early Irish banking world' in *Economists and the Irish economy*, ed. A. E. Murphy (Dublin, 1984).
9. King letterbook 1696-8: Trinity College, Dublin, MS 750/1: Johnston, op. cit., chap. 3. 'Archbishop King's diagnosis'.
10. For the most recent and extensive accounts of these episodes, see Irvin Ehrenpreis, *Swift: the man, his works, and the age*, vol. III (1983), 152-313 *passim;* Isolde L. Victory, 'The development of colonial nationalism, 1692-1725', unpublished Ph.D. thesis, T.C.D., 1985, chaps. 5-6.
11. On the crisis of the later 1720s, see Cullen, *Economic history*, pp. 47-51; Ehrenpreis, op. cit., pp. 570-7.
12. James Maculla, *Proposals for a publick coinage of copper half-pence and farthings in the kingdom of Ireland* . . . (Dublin, 1727); a handy (though by no means impartial) survey of the currency debate is found in Sir John Browne, *A Short review of the several pamphlets. that have appeared this sessions on the subject of coin* . . . (Dublin, 1730).
13. Marian Bowley, *Studies in the history of economic theory before 1870* (1973), pp. 19-27.
14. Prior, *List of absentees* (1729), p. 18.
15. Petty, *Verbum sapienti* (published as an appendix to *Political anatomy*, 1691) in *Economic writings*, I, 113.
16. John Locke, *Some considerations of the consequences of the lowering of interest, and raising the value of money* (2nd edn., 1696), pp. 14, 21-2, 33-42.
17. Davenant is notable for his use of analogies between the circulation of the blood and the circulation of money, esp. in *Discourses on the public revenues, and on the trade of England* (1698). 'Davenant on Trade' is one of the four economic titles in the catalogue for the sale of the Berkeley family library by Leigh and Sotheby in June 1796; QQ. 484 and 590 perhaps echo Davenant on circulation. Davenant is cited as an authority in Prior, *List of absentees*, pp. 62-3, and in Dobbs, *Essay on trade*, part II, p. 14.
18. Prior, *List of absentees*, pp. 19-20: the passage is probably based on Locke, *Some Considerations*, p. 21.
19. Dobbs, *Essay on trade*, part II, pp. 18-20.
20. On Irish currency in the seventeenth and eighteenth centuries, see Johnston, op. cit., chap. 6, and further Cullen, *Economic history*, *pp. 41-7*.
21. [Daniel Webb], *An enquiry into the reasons of the decay of credit, trade and manufactures in Ireland* (Dublin, 1735) proposed issuing £30,000 of notes bearing interest at 3% p.a. for 21 years to help industrious artizans and tradesmen.
22. Prior, *List of absentees*, p. 22.

Patrick Kelly

23. Richard A. Lester, *Monetary experiments: early American and recent Scandanavian* (Princeton, N.J., 1939), chaps. 3-4.

24. For Rhode Island issues, ibid, pp. 8-9, 66, 93-4; Berkeley's comments, QQ. 240, 247, 251-2, 449. Om. Q., I, 212.

25. For early American writings on paper-money, see Joseph Dorfman, *The economic mind in American civilization* (2 vols., 1947), chap. 9.

26. 'The ordinary means . . . to increase our wealth and treasure is by *Forraign Trade*, wherein wee must ever observe this rule; to sell more to strangers yearly than wee consume of theirs in value': Thoman Mun, *England's treasure by forraign trade* (1664) reprinted in *Early English Tracts on Commerce*, ed. J.R. McCulloch (reprint, Cambridge, 1953), p. 125.

27. Cf. Q. 108: 'Whether there be not a great difference between Ireland and Holland? And whether foreign commerce without which one could not subsist be necesary for the other?', and Q. 140: 'whether it be not madness in a poor nation to imitate a rich one?'

28. Berkeley was equally concerned with the need to eradicate the vanity, idleness, and ignorance of the Protestant gentry, see QQ. 332, 379, 346, 201.

29. E.g., T.W. Hutchison, 'Berkeley's *Querist* and its place in the economic thought of the eighteenth century', *British Journal for the Philosophy of Science*, 4 (1953), 304; such also is the implicit approach of Vickers, op. cit., chap. 8.

30. Cf. Locke, *Some Considerations*, pp. 69-77.

31. Joseph A. Schumpeter, *History of economic analysis* (1954), pp. 288-9; for Schumpeter metallism represents tying the value of money to that of some other commodity, the opposite, namely cartalism, represents a money not covered by any form of backing.

32. This judgement scarcely suggests that great familiarity with Law's *Money and trade considered* (1705) that modern commentators assume; Law expressly states (p.85) that notes are to be issued 'on Land Security, the Debt not exceeding one half, or two Thirds of the Value'.

33. Schumpeter, op. cit., p. 289.

34. Locke, *Some Considerations*, pp. 75-6, esp, 'the value of the Pledges being still sufficient, as constantly encreasing with the Plenty of the Commodity'.

35. Cf. ibid, pp. 31-2; Locke indeed is a rather unusual case of a theoretical metallist in that he considers the value of gold and silver as money to derive from the 'universal consent of Mankind' to use them as such, and not from any non-monetary uses which the precious metals may also have.

36. For this debate see Istvan Hont, 'The "rich country — poor country" debate in Scottish classical political economy' in *Wealth and Virtue*, edd. I. Hont and M. Ignatieff (Cambridge, 1983). Hont suggests (pp. 290-1) that the publication of the Glasgow edn. of *The querist* in 1751 was probably connected with this controversy.

116

The clash on semantics in Berkeley's *Notebook A*

by Bertil Belfrage

INTRODUCTION

Eighty years ago Theodor Lorenz published his famous paper on Berkeley's *Philosophical notebooks*.[1] In it he observed that the manuscript volume (BL Add. MS. 39305) consisted of two notebooks bound together: *Notebook A* and *Notebook B*.[2] Lorenz was convinced that these had been bound in the wrong chronological order.[3] Thence arose the 80 year old tradition on how to interpret the *Notebooks*. I have recently examined all major arguments concerning the order and dating of the *Notebooks* that have been presented within this long tradition. I found all these arguments to be inconclusive and the problems to be improperly formulated.[4] In this paper, I take the first constructive step towards an alternative reading of the *Notebooks*, concentrating on *Notebook A*.

I intend to show that there was an important change in Berkeley's intellectual development sometime towards the end of 1707 and beginning of 1708. My thesis is that this change divides the entries in *Notebook A* into two blocks: one expressing an early Lockean view, the other a different—may I call it a Berkeleian?—position. I refer to the earlier block as 'the Lockean entries'—though Locke should in no way be taken as responsible for their contents—and to the other block as 'the later entries'. They correlate approximately with the following groups of entries (the first entry of *Notebook A* being numbered as entry No. 400):[5]

The Lockean entries (400-696) — The later entries (697-888)

I argue my thesis in two steps. First, (1) I present the controversy that, according to my theory, made Berkeley change his view. Then, (2) I trace the clash in *Notebook A* between the early standpoint and the later one. Finally, I observe some consequences of my Clash Hypothesis.[6]

I: THE 'OF INFINITES' CONTROVERSY

Berkeley read his 'Of Infinites' paper before the Dublin Philosophi-

117

Bertil Belfrage

cal Society on 19 November 1707.[7] It has not hitherto been observed that this paper could have generated a great controversy. To a modern reader it probably appears a purely academical discourse concerning some mathematical subtleties. But when read in the light of David Berman's recent studies on Irish philosophy, we may be confident that it was received as an extremely controversial paper, relevant to issues far outside the narrow field of mathematics.[8] Berman docs not mention the paper, but he provides us with the following dramatic background information.

The first radical Irish Lockean was John Toland whose book *Christianity not mysterious* ... (1696) was burnt in 1697 'by the common hangman, and it was moved by someone in the Committee on religion in the Irish House of Commons "that Mr. *Toland* himself should be burnt".'[9] He was able to escape to London, but the next Irish heretic was less fortunate: five years after the official burning of Toland's book, Thomas Emlyn was imprisoned for more than two years for his rationalistic approach to theological issues.[10] Two of the most powerful critics of Toland and Emlyn were William King, Archbishop of Dublin, and Peter Browne then (i.e. in 1707) Provost at Trinity College in Dublin.[11]

It should be noted that both King and Browne were elected members of the council of the Dublin Philosophical Society one week before the meeting where Berkeley read his 'Of Infinites' before that society.[12] The President of the Society was none other than the Earl of Pembroke to whom John Locke had dedicated his *Essay*, and to whom George Berkeley later dedicated his *Principles*.[13] We do not know who were present at that meeting, but one may assume an audience of educated Irish Anglicans well aware of the Toland and Emlyn controversies. My conjecture is that they made Berkeley realize that the Lockean theory of meaning from which he argued in his 'Of Infinites' led to consequences which they found quite unacceptable. It is possible to reconstruct some of these consequences from Berkeley's own manuscripts.

In one of the most radical Lockean entries in *Notebook A* (No. 696), Berkeley says:

I   ... Let him [my Reader] not regard my Words any otherwise than
as occasions of bringing into his mind determin'd ideas so far as they
fail of this they are Gibberish, Jargon & deserve not the name of
Language ...[14]

One can easily understand what unacceptable theological conse-

118

quences this view implies, if we read it with that passage in the Scripture which Berkeley examines in both the manuscripts written a few months after the meeting: the so-called first sermon and the *Manuscript introduction* (often called the *Draft introduction* to the *Principles*).[15] The same passage had been used by Browne in his attack against Toland in 1697.[16] Maybe he used it against Berkeley ten years later as well. It is the following passage, patently void of any descriptive meaning:[17]

> We are told that the Good Things which God hath prepared for them that love him are such as Eye hath not seen nor Ear heard nor hath it enter'd into the Heart of Man to conceive. (MI 36)

Berkeley says:

> who is there that can say they [these Words] bring into his Mind clear and determinate Ideas or in Truth any Ideas at all (MI 36, 36a).

As the Pauline promise did not 'bring into his Mind' any 'clear and determinate Ideas', the unacceptable consequence of what I take to be the last radically Lockean entry in *Notebook A* (No. 696) is that: such propositions in the Scripture 'are Gibberish, Jargon & deserve not the name of Language'. I take it that Berkeley would regard such a consequence as a *reductio ad absurdum* of his own early Lockean position. He started to qualify this position at once, as we can see in the manuscripts that he wrote at this time.

Already in his first sermon he officially denied his early Lockean position. The clash between it and the 'Of Infinites' is remarkable indeed. The two substantial points that Berkeley makes in the paper were explicitly denied in the sermon—less than two months after the meeting where he had read the paper.[18] ''Tis plain to me', Berkeley says in the paper, 'we ought to use no sign without an idea answering it' (pp. 235-236), whereas in the sermon he presents a demonstration in which the reference to infinite eternal bliss—that 'we have no idea of'—is crucial to the whole argument (pp . 11, 13). And in the sermon he admits that this 'infinite' is 'beyond the compass of our imagination' (p.13), but the main point in the 'Of Infinites' is that an argument based on such a concept of infinity is invalid.

His new discovery in the *Manuscript introduction* was that terms in non-cognitive discourse can be used for (one or more of) the following ends: (a) 'the raising of some Passion', (b) 'the putting the Mind in some particular Disposition', and (c) 'the exciting to or deterring from an Action' (MI 40, 40a). Thence emerged the first emotive theory of meaning in the history of ideas, probably as a result of the 'Of Infinites' controversy.[19] Before the meeting, he accepted the Lockean 'axiom', '*No* word to be used without an idea' (422, my emphasis).[20] His new position, after the *Manuscript introduction*, was that we can use language for other ends than for strictly descriptive purposes.[21] This was the first step, as I see it, towards a new Berkeleian semantics.

II.   THE CLASH ON SEMANTICS IN NOTEBOOK A

The doctrinal clash between the 'Of Infinites' and the first sermon concerned the proper use of terms in a valid demonstration. As there is an extensive discussion regarding the proper use of numbers in a mathematical demonstration throughout *Notebook A*, I concentrate on (i) the concept of number and (ii) the nature of demonstration with the end in view of identifying the same clash on semantics in this *Notebook* as there is between the 'Of Infinites' and the first sermon.

(i) *The concept of number*

(a) Numbers denote ideas (in the Lockean entries)

The concept of number in the Lockean entries is connected with a new approach to geometry that Berkeley developed in opposition to traditional geometry (428, 432, 457, 458, 481, 511, 515, 525, 575). Extended objects were defined in terms of the number and arrangement of 'indivisibles' (462-463, 510) or 'points'. He says that:

> those lines [are] equal wch contain an equal number of points (516)
>
> I can mean (for my part) nothing else by equal Triangles than Triangles containing equal numbers of Points (530)
>
> Etc.

This made him develop a most primitive concept of number—as long as he accepted the semantic rule that terms which do not

The clash on semantics in Berkeley's *Notebook A*

denote particular ideas are empty, meaningless, terms. And this rule was accepted as an 'axiom' in the Lockean entries (417, 421, 422, 448, 576-576a, 584, 638, 696, cf. 488, 528, 595, 639). I observe two consequences of this view.

A number is taken to denote particular things 'conceiv'd . . . as consisting of parts wch may be distinctly & successively perceiv'd' (460, cf. 475).[22] As extended objects, such as a line, were supposed to consist of an exact number of points (469, 470, 510, 511, 558), only natural numbers could be used to describe the correct size of an extended object. Consequently, he says, 'there are no incommensurables, no surds' (469). This was, for instance, the reason why he concluded: 'the Pythagoric Theorem is false' (500).[23]

Another consequence was that numbers for quantities too small (488) or too big (655) 'to be comprehended or perceiv'd all at once' (475, cf. 460) were rejected as meaningless conceptions.

(b) Terms can be used for instrumental, non-descriptive purposes

Berkeley took an important step in his intellectual development, when he observed the possibility of using terms emotively in the *Manuscript introduction*. But this was only the first step, I argue, in an interesting development. In *Alciphron* VII, for instance, we read:

> that there may be another use of words, besides that of marking and suggesting distinct ideas, to wit, the influencing our conduct and actions; which may be done either by forming rules for us to act by, or by raising certain passions, dispositions, and emotions in our minds. (Sect. 5, 3rd ed.)

But those 'rules for us to act by' now include 'numberless rules and theorems directing men how to act, and explaining phenomena throughout the Mechanics and mathematical philosophy' (sect. 7, 3rd ed.). So expanded, only *one* form of non-descriptive use of language is properly called *emotive* usage. In scientific enquiry it is more appropriate to speak about an *instrumental* use of language. Terms used instrumentally do *not* denote ideas; 'for instance', he says:

> the algebraic mark, which denotes the root of a negative square, hath its use in logistic operations, although it be impossible to form an idea of any such quantity. (Sect. 14, 3rd ed.)

121

I argue, this view that terms can be used for instrumental, non-descriptive, purposes caused him to change his view on the concept of number in the *Notebooks*.

(c) Numbers do not denote ideas (in the later entries)

In the Lockean entries even numbers were supposed to denote ideas, as we have seen. But in the later entries Berkeley emphasizes concerning 'the Nature of Numbers' that 'I regard *not* the Idea... but the Names' (761, cf. 758, 759, 760, my emphasis) — just as he declares in *Principles* 122 that in arithmetic 'we regard not the *things* but the *signs*'; and signs used in a mathematical calculus 'do not suggest ideas of particular things to our minds' (*ibid.*).

The strict referential meaning required in the Lockean entries is replaced by an instrumental use of mathematical signs in the later entries (765, 767, 768, 803). The curious idea that very high numbers cannot be accepted, because we are unable to imagine objects above (or below) a certain size, is now rejected. He even uses high numbers (761) and 'Imaginary roots' (764)—which cannot possibly denote an image-picture of some particular number of things— in order to illustrate the nature of numbers. This is a complete clash with the Lockean entries. And, I argue, there is a similar clash concerning the nature of demonstration.

(ii) *The nature of demonstration*

(a) A valid demonstration is 'confined barely to our own Ideas' (in the Lockean entries)

Convinced, in the Lockean entries, that 'all our knowlege & contemplation is confin'd barely to our own Ideas' (606, see also 521, 522, 531, 539), Berkeley found it 'absurd to talk or make propositions about' that which we have no idea of (354, 417, 421). Therefore, in 'legitimate Demonstrations' we are required never to 'go beyond our Ideas' (584, 638). At this stage he did not, as he puts it, accept 'consequences of Words as Something different from consequences of Ideas' (595). Therefore, since such terms as 'congruence' and 'identity' do not denote any particular object, for instance, he rejected them as being empty and (therefore) useless terms (528-529, 592). Thus confined to the 'constant train of Particular Ideas' to which his Solitary Man was bound to restrict his enquiry, he rejected the tools for accepting any truth that 'consists in the joyning

& separating of signs' (554).[24] It is hard to understand how he could formulate any language at all or perform any theoretical demonstration, as long as no terms other than descriptive were accepted.

(b) Demonstrations taken as convenient scientific instruments

In *Principles* 118-119 Berkeley attacks the view that terms in a mathematical calculus have referential meaning; his own view is presented in *Principles* 120-122. 'Number [,] being defined a *collection of units*' (120), is of the wrong logical category to denote any particular thing. 'The theories therefore in arithmetic'—expressed by such 'numeral names and figures'—'have nothing at all for their object' (120). Demonstrations in mathematics are described as a 'computing in signs'(121)—or as 'logistic operations' in which such terms as '$\sqrt{-1}$' work perfectly well, 'although it be impossible to form an idea of any such quantity' (*Alciphron* VII 14).

The difference between a mere game and a scientific calculus is that the latter is supposed to work by 'explaining phenomena' (*Alciphron* VII 7) in a proper way. Thus it is required of the results of a mathematical calculus that they apply to 'whatever particular things men had need to compute' (*Principles* 122). In that sense a mathematical calculus (in the broad sense in which Berkeley used the term) is 'subordinate to practice' (120).

(c) There is 'no comparing of ideas' in a mathematical demonstration (in the later entries)

In the later entries Berkeley had come to the position he was to hold in his published works. Whereas he was confined in his early concretism to what he styles 'consequences of Ideas' (595), he now emphasizes that there is 'no comparing of Ideas' in demonstrations performed in arithmetic and algebra (767-768). 'Take away the signs from Arithmetic & Algebra, & pray w^t remains?' (767, 750, cf. 881), he asks rhetorically. Now he has come to look upon a mathematical demonstration as a mere 'computing in signs' to use his term in *Principles* 121.

When we apply the result of our scientific enquiries to phenomena, however, it is required—on this basic, ontological level—that the terms we use have descriptive meaning. On this level we should always, as Berkeley puts it, be able to 'look beneath the words & Uncover [our] Ideas' (736, 719, 737, 740, 748, 816, PI 21 ff.).

Bertil Belfrage

I have now presented evidence in support of my theory that there is a clash in *Notebook A* dividing the entries into two blocks, the one contradicting the other on important issues. If the theory is correct, then what are its consequences?

One difficulty in the traditional reversed-order approach to the *Notebooks* (according to which all of *B* is earlier than all of *A*) is that the Lockean entries are supposed to mark the climax of Berkeley's intellectual development. But how can we then explain that here—in this very part of *Notebook A* where he was supposed to have reached his most mature position—he all of a sudden starts contradicting some of his most fundamental doctrines? Some scholars were particularly shocked by the empiricist concept of mind that he developed in the Lockean entries. He says, for example:

> +Mind is a congeries of Perceptions. Yake away Perceptions & you take away the Mind put the Perceptions & you put the mind (580)

Those scholars who focused on the view expressed in the *Principles* argued that the view Berkeley published was his real view all the time: he did not mean what he said in the so-called Humean entries in *Notebook A*.[25] Other scholars who were more in line with the strict empiricist view argued that his real view was the one found in the Lockean entries, whereas he did not mean what he said in the *Principles*.[26] Who is right? If Berkeley is allowed to not mean what he says in the one place, why not in the other as well?

A series of interrelated hypotheses arose in order to understand this difficulty, such as the Commentary Hypothesis, the Black List Hypothesis, and the Error Hypothesis.[27] They were supposed to explain both why he included views in his *Notebooks* that he did not approve of, and how to identify those 'scrap-heap entries'. I have recently argued that all these hypotheses fail.[28] If we try to create one doctrine out of two incompatible contexts, then surely the result will be one very confused picture. My own view is very simple. He did not contradict himself at all. He argued his Lockean position with a logical consistency close to rigidity. But after the clash on semantics, he developed a quite different view. The contradictions mark a significant change in Berkeley's philosophical development, as I see it.

There are, however, entries of a very different kind in these *Notebooks*. There are tentative, searching entries where he asks: was

The clash on semantics in Berkeley's *Notebook A*

I right in this, could that be the case? There are those where he formulates the result or defends it against various criticisms. But there are also entries where he quotes other philosophers for later consideration. There could very well be cases, therefore, where he included in his *Notebooks* something that was not an explicit formulation of his own doctrine at that time. But the reliability of an entry has to be argued from case to case on scholarly grounds. To state that Berkeley did not mean what he says in those entries which simply do not fit in with our own interpretation would be to open the field to complete arbitrariness.

It should be carefully noted, however, that my hypothesis has not yet been sufficiently established. I have only dealt with Berkeley's development on semantics in *Notebook A* in this paper. In order to establish a Clash Hypothesis, a series of clashes on other subjects must also be recorded. And in order to draw any conclusions concerning the classical problem on the order of the *Notebooks*, *Notebook B* has also to be carefully examined. What I claim to have done in this paper is to have contributed the *first* piece of evidence towards this broader project.[29]

Notes

1. Theodor Lorenz, 'Weitere Beiträge zur Lebensgeschichte George Berkeleys (IV)', *Archiv für Geschichte der Philosophie*, Band XVIII (1905), p. 551 ff.
2. The two notebooks were referred to as A and B for the first time in G. A. Johnston, *The development of Berkeley's philosophy* (1925), reprinted New York: Russell & Russell. 1965. See p. 22n. A. C. Fraser found the manuscript and published it as the *Commonplace book* in his 1874 edition of Berkeley's *Works*. A. A. Luce renamed it the *Philosophical Commentaries* (see note 5, below).
3. In Lorenz 1905 (see note 1), p. 554, he argued, however, that the end of *B* includes the very last entries.
4. Bertil Belfrage, 'The order and dating of Berkeley's *Notebooks*' in *George Berkeley (1685-1985). Revue Internationale de Philosophie*. No. 154 (1985) pp. 196-214.
5. I follow the numbering of the entries introduced in A. A. Luce (ed.). *George Berkeley. Philosophical Commentaries generally called the Commonplace Book*. London: Thomas Nelson and Sons Ltd. 1944. For a new numbering, see my edition of Berkeley's *Philosophical Notebooks* (forthcoming).
6. It is improper to speak about *the* clash. If I am right, there is not one but a series of clashes with regard to different issues and on different levels which took place over some period of time. But I refer to this complex event by that simple term, now concentrating on the clash on semantics.
7. Published in *Works*. vol. 4. pp. 235-238. For the dating, see BL Sloane Papers, Add. MS. 4812, folio 30.
8. David Berman, 'Enlightenment and Counter-Enlightenment in Irish Philosophy', *Archiv für Geschichte der Philosophie*. Band 64 (1982), pp. 148-165.
9. Berman 1982 (see note 8), p. 152.
10. *Ibid.*
11. *Ibid.*

125

Bertil Belfrage

12. See K. Theodore Hoppen, *The common scientist in the seventeenth century: a study of the Dublin Philosophical Society 1683-1708.* London: Routledge & Kegan Paul, 1970, p. 193.

13. Hoppen 1970 (see note 12), p. 192.

14. The entry is quoted in its first stratum.

15. The sermon is published in *Works*, vol. 7, pp. 9-15, the other manuscript in Bertil Belfrage (ed.), *George Berkeley. Manuscript Introduction.* Oxford: Doxa, 1985.

16. See David Berman, 'Berkeley's semantic revolution' (forthcoming).

17. 'MI' is short for the *Manuscript Introduction* (see note 15). References are to my numbering of the sections.—The quotation is a conflation of two passage (see my Editor's Introduction to the MI).

18. The sermon is dated 'College chappell. Sunday evening. January 11, 1707/8'. See *Works*, vol. 7, p. 15.

19. See my 'Berkeley's emotive theory of meaning (1708)' (forthcoming).

20. See also entries 448, 488, 584, 595, 638, 639, 696.

21. He was aware of non-cognitive discourse in, for instance, entry No. 584. But he had no theory for non-descriptive uses of language at first, if we may judge from the *Notebooks.*

22. Probably 'number' is defined operationally by reference to the act of counting perceivable parts of particular objects.

23. The absurdity is that 'One square cannot be double of another'; if so, the sides would be in the ratio of 1 to $\sqrt{2}$; but $\sqrt{2}$ is rejected in entry 469, hence also the Pythagoric Theorem that can lead to this alledgedly absurd consequence.

24. See MI 48, 52-54.

25. A. A. Luce, 'Berkeley's *Commonplace Book* — its date, purpose, structure, and marginal signs', *Hermathena* 47 (1932), p. 110. See also A. A. Luce, *Berkeley and Malebranche. A study in the origin of Berkeley's thought* (1934). Reprint Oxford: Oxford University Press, 1967, p. 105; and A. A. Luce. *'The dialectic of immaterialism. An account of the making of Berkeley's Principles.* London: Hodder and Stoughton. 1963. p. 173. cf. p. 24 ff.

26. C. M. Turbayne argued in 'Berkeley's two concepts of mind' in Gale W. Engle and Gabriele Taylor (eds.), *Berkeley's Principles of human knowledge: critical studies.* Belmont, California: Wadsworth Publishing Company, Inc., 1968, p. 25, that the Humean entries express the 'secret doctrine' that Berkeley intended to publish in Part II of the *Principles.* To interpret sect. 27 of the *Principles* literally is a mistake, according to Turbayne (p. 29): here, Berkeley speaks of mind and spirit in a metaphorical way (pp. 26-28).

27. The Commentary Hypothesis was first presented in A. A. Luce, 'The purpose and the date of Berkeley's *Commonplace Book'*, *Proceedings of the Royal Irish Academy*, vol. XLVIII, Sec. C. No. 7, Dublin 1943, pp. 275-279. It is further developed in Luce 1963 (see note 25), Chapter 2.

The Black List Hypothesis was first presented in Luce 1932 (see note 25), p. 109 f. It was argued in detail in Luce 1944 (see note 5), p. xxvi, and applied in Luce 1963 (see note 25 above), pp. 8ff., 24, 82 *et passim.*

For a discussion from the Error Hypothesis, see Luce 1963, Chapter 1.

28. In 'A new approach to Berkeley's *Philosophical Notebooks'* (forthcoming).

29. I am grateful to David Berman and Robert McKim for comments on an earlier version of this essay.

Pleasure and pain versus ideas in Berkeley

by Geneviève Brykman

To scrutinize pleasure and pain as opposed to ideas in Berkeley is a way to question the status of *passivity* in his works. It is generally admitted that ideas are passive in Berkeley; by contrast the mind is stressed rather as active, though the human mind should be said to be passive as well as active. From an analysis of Berkeley's statements about pleasure and pain in the early works[1], I: we shall bring out what exactly mind-passivity is as contrasted with the ideas-passivity; II: we shall exhibit how the statement from Philonous about the mind as 'altogether passive' in perception is only a trick; III: we shall bring out how the pleasure and pain polarity is the core of spirit for any living creature to whom 'exteriority' is the objective side of a fictitious ideal balance between pleasure and pain. The world is not chiefly an exterior being but something distinct which may either gratify or hurt.

I. THE MIND-PASSIVITY AS CONTRASTED WITH THE IDEAS-PASSIVITY.

Roughly speaking, mind is active and ideas are passive in Berkeley. Roughly speaking indeed. Such a statement is only able to justify Berkeley's purpose: immaterialism is not to change things into ideas but ideas into things. We shall not at present challenge the statement that ideas are passive and shall focus first on one single question: How far is it possible to say that a mind is active? Strickly speaking, the supposition of a God as *Actus purus*[2] is the only way to give a meaning to this statement. Of that Berkeley was so well aware that he describes the human mind, from the *Notebooks* to the Letters to Johnson[3], as a being which should be considered as 'passive as well as active'. Or to say it in another way there is 'something passive in our soul'; as Johnson said, 'we are purely passive in the reception of our ideas'.[4]

What exactly is the passive reception of ideas? One should observe that the expression 'altogether passive' is used in two ways in the *Three dialogues*. It is used in the *First dialogue* to qualify the human mind;[5] then it is used in quite a different way in the *Third dialogue*

127

Geneviève Brykman

to qualify ideas,[6] when the word 'idea' is used in the narrow Berkeleyan sense settled in the *Notebooks* and the *Principles*.[7]

—That ideas are inactive should be more clearly exhibited by two words:

> ideas are both *passive* and *inert*, Berkeley says more than once;[8] which means that ideas: A) as passive, are acted upon, are suffering actions from outside; B) as inert, they are void of any power of action, motion or resistance.

—The description of a finite mind as passive is obviously different:

> the finite mind is passive as far as it is acted upon. It is suffering actions from God's initiative, but it is never inert, otherwise it would be annihilated. The very nature of spirit is to be active.[9] Thus the nature of a finite spirit is to be acted upon by God without being inert at all. Contrary to the well known statement of Philonous that we are 'altogether passive in perception', Berkeley everywhere else states that, though there is actually something passive in our souls, we should say that 'while (we) exist, or have any idea, (we) are eternally constantly willing', the acquiescing in the represent state is willing (N.B. 791). This is another way to say that, unlike ideas, finite spirits are passive without being inert at all. Acquiescing or reacting is the only way for creatures to carry out a desire for happiness and security which should be the ground of all moral concern.[10]

II. IS THE MIND 'ALTOGETHER PASSIVE' IN PERCEPTION?

II.1. We have just answered this question. However Philonous's statements in the *First dialogue* gave rise to comments that one cannot leave aside. We shall take another look at such arguments. In a nutshell, Philonous's arguments, in the *First dialogue*, are mostly tricky devices to get Hylas in trouble without asserting Berkeley's immaterialism as such.

It is true that, in the *First dialogue*, Philonous makes use of arguments for an immaterialism in the broad sense of the word: an immaterialism which might have been asserted by any 'new philosopher' from the time of Descartes. As P. Bayle rightly noticed in his *Dictionary*,[11] every argument by which the new philosophers show that secondary qualities do not exist could have been brought against the primary qualities as well. Philonous uses such arguments, which could have been those of Bayle, Foucher or Malebranche. But, as Berkeley explicitly said in the *Principles* § 15: 'This

128

Pleasure and pain versus ideas in Berkeley

method of arguing doth not so much prove that there is no extension or colour in an outward object, as that we do not know by sense which is the true extension or colour of the object.' As we know from the *Preface* of the work, the aim of the *Three dialogues* was 'to treat more clearly and fully' of certain principles laid down in the first (and only) part of the *Principles*. But Berkeley had gone further, saying he would place these principles 'in a new light'. The new light was obscurity, so far as in the *First dialogue* Philonous has been considered by commentators as thoroughly representing Berkeley the philosopher, without much concern for Berkeley the religious educator. Now, whereas a 'killing blow' is of no use to an educator, a basic rule should be 'to make truth glide insensibly into the soul'.[12] Hence to make truth acceptable, Philonous adopts in the *First dialogue* some views which are obviously Lockeian and which contrast, at the very least, with his own tenets in the *Third dialogue*.

From this preliminary warning we shall focus on two arguments of Philonous in the *First dialogue*, which both have to do with the distinction between the passivity of ideas and the passivity of spirits: 1) that we have 'a simple and uncompounded idea' of intense heat and/or pain; 2) that we are 'altogether passive' in the very perception of a smell or a colour.

II.2. *The heat/pain argument:* The argument states that an intense heat, as it is in a vehement pain, shows that heat is in the mind where pain is;[13] or to put it in another way, as Philonous exactly said, we have one 'simple and uncompounded idea' of pain and heat, therefore heat is in the mind where pain is. This argument requires three observations:

1. To say that we have 'one simple and uncompounded idea' of pain and heat is *to speak along Locke's lines on simple ideas (Essay* II, ch. VII). To Locke, pleasure and pain are two names for the way in which all our other ideas are more or less pleasant or unpleasant on a scale where the different degrees of pleasure and unpleasure are responsible for the various names we give to our affections. But Locke insists that, in spite of their peculiar property to be joined to all other ideas, pleasure and pain are nevertheless *ideas*.
2. *Let us remember a clever comment by Tipton* on this heat/pain argument;[14] that one case of intense heat cannot allow extension to every sensory experience. Ordinarily to the question: 'What do I feel?', I can make this double answer: (x) — I feel some warm exterior thing, which experience I describe as the experience of a *quality* of the thing; — (y) I dimly feel a pleasant *sensation* in my body, which I ascribe to my private experience. The answer (x) or (y) is relative to the attention we

pay either to (x) or to (y). In the case of a vehement pain, we cannot attend to anything else but this pain. This kind of experience is actually unusual and that statement about a 'simple uncompounded idea' to which Philonous alludes is groundless. Philonous unduly makes of the exception the rule.

3. On this particular argument, *Berkeley's opinion should not be identified with Philonous's one.* We have the clear statement in the Notebook that pleasure and pain attend more or less the whole range of our sensible ideas. These two basic affects give rise to all sorts of desires, passions and actions; moreover they are the very principles of the boundary between an inward and an outward world: in *Notebook* A 692 Berkeley asks: 'How comes it that some ideas are confessedly allow'd by all to be onely in the mind and others as generally taken to be without the mind, if according to you, all are equally and only in the mind?' Here follows an answer which is quite different from the Philonous's heat/pain argument: 'because that in proportion to the pleasure and pain, ideas are attended with desire, aversion and other actions which include volition, now volition is by all granted to be in spirit.'

It is true that Locke here paved the way with Book II, ch. VII, of the *Essay*. This chapter is altogether concerned with an odd kind of simple ideas which have this peculiar property of being conveyed to the mind by all the ways of sensation and reflection. At the very outset come pleasure and pain. 'Delight or uneasiness', Locke says, 'one or other of them join themselves to almost all our ideas both of sensation and reflection.'

To return to Berkeley we should observe that the *Essay* on vision is much concerned with pleasure and pain, on a level with 'the most inward passion' of the soul.[15] Without pleasure and pain it would be impossible to bring up the universal language by which visual ideas are a regular suggestion of a tactual experience to come.[16] Again, the first section of the *Principles*, though not so explicitly as the *Notebooks* and *Essay* on vision, makes pleasure and unpleasure qualifications of the three kinds of ideas that are mentioned in the survey made of the objects of knowledge. It is clearly stated that, through pleasure or unpleasure, sensible things excite various passions of 'love, hatred, joy, grief and so forth'.[17]

On this score of pleasure and pain, a considerable difference between Locke and Berkeley is that from 'simple ideas of both sensation and reflexion' in the *Essay concerning human understanding*, II, ch. VII, pleasure and pain are no more ideas at all in Berkeley. They are the different names for one single experience the individual self has at once to be 'I', 'to exist', 'to endure' and 'to will'. An experience which is more like a *conatus* than like an idea of any kind whatever.

We should conclude that whereas ideas are in the mind not by way of modes or attributes, but by the way of *objects* for the mind[18] pleasure and pain are in the mind by way of *modes* without which there would not be any thought nor any finite subject at all.

II.3. *The 'altogether passive' argument.* Here again, in the *First dialogue*

Pleasure and pain versus ideas in Berkeley

is a trick of Philonous which is easily foiled by remembering the continual statements of Berkeley: 1) that the human mind is passive and active;[19] 2) that that very acquiescing in the present state is willing.[20] A close look at the argument will show that Philonous is leading Hylas into a trap. Indeed Philonous compels Hylas to an odd abstraction by asking the following questions;[21] in smelling this particular smell, am I not altogether passive? in perceiving white rather than any other colour on this flower, am I not altogether passive? This particular smell, the white colour in the flower are abstractions from the whole of a concrete experience. Hence Philonous is at ease to conclude: 'Since therefore you are in the very perception of light and colour altogether passive, what has become of that action you were speaking of as an ingredient in every sensation?'[22] Only if you admit the above abstraction can you say that perception of light and colour is altogether passive. 'From *your own concessions*', Philonous concludes, perception of light and colour, because inactive, may exist in an unthinking substance.

This concession, however, was a momentary episode. Neither Philonous nor Hylas considers that a perception is really altogether passive. Thus Philonous goes on, more fairly to Hylas: 'since you distinguish the *active* and *passive* in every perception you must do it in that of pain. But how is it possible that pain, be it as little active as you please, should exist in an unperceiving substance? In short, do but consider the point, and then confess ingenuously, whether light and colours, taste, sounds etc . . are not all equally passions or sensations in the soul'.[23]

Here again Philonous uses the Lockeian identification of pleasure and pain with sensible ideas, to state that they are all 'equally passions or sensations in the soul'. However, it is thoroughly wrong to equate here the *passivity of pain or pleasure as modes* of consciousness, with the passivity of sensible ideas as objects for consciousness. One may observe that Philonous, in the *First dialogue*, leaves no stone unturned. Previously, he has described the relation of pleasure and pain to ideas more in accordance with Berkeley's direct statements. Let us now examine this peculiar relation of pleasure and pain to ideas in Berkeley.

III. THE RELATION OF PLEASURE/UNPLEASURE TO IDEAS.

What reason can be given for the distinction made by philosophers between primary and secondary qualities, Hylas had asked, at the end of the review of sensible qualities which had exhibited that they exist in the mind.[24] Philonous had answered: 'Among the reasons which may be assigned for this, it seems probable that pleasure and pain, being rather annexed to the latter than the former may be one. Heat and cold, tastes and smells, have something more vividly pleasing or disagreeable than the ideas of extension, figure and motion affect us with. And it being too visibly absurd to hold that pain or pleasure can be in an unperceiving substance, men are more easily weaned from believing the external existence of the secondary than the primary qualities (. . .) But after all, there is no rational ground for that distinction; for surely an *indifferent* sensation is as truly a sensation as one more pleasing or painful; and consequently should not anymore than they be supposed to exist in an unthinking subject'.[25]

Contrary to what he has said before about the 'simple and uncompounded idea' of pain/heat, Philonous here analyses ideas as diversely modified by various degrees of pleasure and pain. Such a description brings forth, in accordance with the *Notebooks* and the *Essay* on vision, how exteriority is conceived by Berkeley as the apparent indifference of some perceptions which are not directly involved in the preservation of the finite sensible creature.

However it should be stressed that indifference is only apparent.[26] Hylas had previously tried a distinction between heat as a *quality* in the object, and pain as a *feeling* in the subject, by suggesting an *indolence* which would be a privation of both pleasure and pain. Such an indolence should have worked to settle the quality of the object as independent from the consciousness we have of it. Hylas relies on this score on an analysis already made by Cordemoy, Malebranche or Saint Evremond.[27] Let us only go back again to Locke, whose *Essay* was the masterpiece for Berkeley.

Delight or uneasiness, we are told in the *Essay*, 'one or other of them *join themselves* at almost all our ideas both of sensation and reflection, and there is scarce any affection of our sense from without, any retired thought of our mind within, which is not able to produce in us pleasure or pain' (II, VII, § 2). That delight and uneasiness 'join themselves' to almost all other ideas is immediately corrected in the next section; as long as they are not yet said to be *ideas*, they seem able to qualify ideas as they are in Berkeley's *Principles*. However, Locke was obviously aware of the Spinozistic flavour there was in saying that all ideas, of any kind whatever, are pleasant or unpleasant. It would be another way to say, as it is actually said in Spinoza's *Ethics*, that 'ideas are not mute pictures on a panel',[28] or that ideas are beliefs and not merely the content of a belief.

Pleasure and pain versus ideas in Berkeley

Hence Locke corrects the statement that delight and uneasiness 'join themselves' to other ideas as follows:

> The infinite wise Author of our being (. .) has been pleased to join to several thoughts and several sensations a perception of delight. If this were wholly separated from all our outward sensations and inward thoughts, we should have no reason to prefer one thought or action to another, negligence to attention, or motion to rest. And so we should neither stir our bodies, nor employ our minds but let our thoughts run adrift, without any direction and design; and suffer the ideas of our minds, like unregarded shadows, to make their appearance there as it happened, without attending to them. (*Essay* II, VII § 3).

This heuristic supposition of our having ideas wholly separated from pleasure and pain is, in one way, quite similar to the description Berkeley gives of our actual observation of objects through a microscope. The *Essay* on vision clearly states that the microscope brings us, as it were, into a new world, where there is no more connection between the visible and the tangible data. By the naked eye we perceive ideas which have a connection with a tactual experience. Thus 'we are taught to foresee what will ensue upon the approach or application of distant objects to the parts of our own body, which much conduceth to its preservation' (N.T.V. 85). Were our eyes turned into microscopes, we should no more be able to make the connection with the tangible and 'have left us only empty amusement of seeing' (N.T.V. 86).

At first sight, it seems as if the connection between pleasure or pain and other ideas in Locke had the function assigned to the connection between visible and tangible ideas in Berkeley. And as in ordinary healthy experience we have a dim awareness of our body and mind, it is worth observing how several times Berkeley says that visual ideas are by themselves 'little taken notice of'.[29] This superficial analogy between pleasure/pain in Locke and visual ideas in Berkeley does not work, however. In the *Essay* on vision sensible experience is described in a way which gives to the tactual data a definite priority: we regard, Berkeley says, 'the objects that environ us in proportion as they are adapted to benefit or injure our own bodies, and thereby produce in our minds the sensation of pleasure or pain. Now bodies operating on our organs, by an immediate application, and the hurt or advantage arising therefrom depending altogether on the tangible, and not at all on the visible qualities of any object; this is a plain reason why those should be regarded by us more than these; and for this end the visive sense seems to have been bestowed on animals, to wit, that by the perception of visible ideas (. .) they may be able to foresee the damage or benefit which is like to ensue upon the application of their own body to this or that body which is at a distance' (N.T.V. 59). That is not saying that visible ideas are void of pleasure and pain; but it brings forward a definite hierarchy of pleasures and pains which was alluded to the Notebook before. Here Berkeley stated that there are two sorts of pleasures: 'the one is ordained as a spur or incitement to somewhat else and has a visible relation and subordination thereto, the other is not' (Notebook A, 852). As long as 'we are chained to a body',[30] the end for which everything else is a means is selfpreservation. Thus visual and auditive ideas, with the associated affects, are hardly used for recreation only.[31] Through pleasure and pain, all our sensible ideas are means for the preservation of one set of tangible ideas.

Because of the early and everlasting connection of visible ideas to the tangible data, it is nearly impossible to enjoy visual data for themselves in Berkeley. However, no idea is indifferent, no idea is void of pleasure or pain; and for this reason ideas, through these two basic affects,[32] give rise to various passions or actions. Berkeley settles the point from the outset, though casually, in the first section of the *Principles*. The tenet that no idea is indifferent was actually better stressed in the Notebook (A. 833):

> It seems there can be no perception, no idea without will, being there are no ideas so indifferent but one had rather have them than annihilation, or annihilation than them; or if there be such an equal ballance there must be an equal mixture of pleasure and pain to cause it; there being no idea perfectly void of all pain and uneasiness but what are preferable to annihilation.

In this note, as in some other casual passages of the published works, it seems rather that pleasure and pain not only qualify ideas but are actually parts or 'ingredients' of them. This description is a trace of Locke's docrine of complex ideas: complex ideas are made up of simple ones or, we are sometimes told, made up of such and such 'ingredients'.[33] Following Locke's description we should have to admit that Berkeley's sensible ideas are complex ideas including: 1) a peculiar sense-datum for each sense — let us call it the *cognitive-ingredient*; 2) an associated ingredient of pleasure or pain which would be the *affective-ingredient*.

However, Berkeley was more sensitive than Locke to the evidence

Pleasure and pain versus ideas in Berkeley

that pleasure and pain are not ideas on a level with the bodily sensations. Thus he usually uses adjectival descriptions: sensible ideas are directly said to be 'pleasant' or 'unpleasant', with no further analysis but the peremptory statement that ideas are 'passive and inert'. The problem left before us then is that the passivity of ideas seems at odds with a power of ideas to affect us.

We would suggest that sensible ideas (or perceptions) are twofold in Berkeley. They are at once things-ideas and affects-ideas, which are two sides of one coin that Berkeley tried to suggest with the expression: 'ideas or sensations'.[34] From this distinction of a cognitive and an affective side of ideas, we should say that among our five organized kinds of sense-data, each idea might be considered as a *thing-idea* and as an *affect-idea*, the proportion of the latter being greater in the 'secondary qualities' than in 'the primary qualities'. This proportion is rather an intensity which (as it is in the case of the heat/pain argument) may become overwhelming to a point which makes the *thing-idea* vanish. We should add that:

(a) — *things-ideas* have this peculiar property of mental states to be 'intentional' i.e. to point out to something else than the mind and body which have them: such are the heat of the poker or the colour of the flower;

(b) — *affects-ideas*, on the other hand, are the relational property of these things-ideas to ourselves. Strictly speaking (which way to speak is missing in Berkeley), it is not pain but painfulness, not pleasure but pleasureableness, which should be the other side of a sensible idea, i.e. a (causal) power to affect us.

One may object that this affective side of the idea is only a way to speak. Ideas do not affect us, only God does. We would answer that the way Berkeley describes the ideas of sense as more vividly present and affecting than the ideas of imagination[35] might compel us to another look at the 'language of the Author of nature'. It may be that we should have to link this language with the 'never enough admired laws of pleasure and pain' that Berkeley speaks of at the end of the *Principles*.[36] This attention to the 'never enough admired laws of pleasure and pain strengthens the demand Berkeley makes everywhere for a theological study of Nature which would overcome mechanical physics. As Hylas stressed, closing the Dialogues with Philonous: 'Things regards us only as they are pleasing or displeasing'.[37]

Geneviève Brykman

Notes

1. By 'early works' we mean the writings (published or not) which were issued before the end of 1713.
2. *Notebook* A, 701, 828, 870.
3. *Notebooks* 286, 362a, 378, 429, 429a, 706, 777, 790, 791, 841— *Correspondence with Johnson,, Works* II, p. 293: *Berkeley to Johnson*, 24 March 1730.
4. *Johnson to Berkeley*, February 5, 1729/30, *Works* II, p. 289.
5. D.H.P. (I), *Works* II, p. 196-197: 'Since you are in the very perception of light and colours altogether passive, what is become of that action you were speaking of, as an ingredient in every sensation?'
6. D.H.P. (III), *Works* II, p. 231: Philonous says that ideas 'are altogether passive' (. . .). 'Ideas are things inactive and perceived, and spirits a sort of beings altogether different from them.'
7. *Notebook A*, 657a, 712, 775; *Principles* § 38-39.
8. *Notebook B*, 228, 230, 427a; A 712. *Principles* § 25, 39, 89, 135-138.
9. *Notebook A*, 437a, 706, 712, 777, 791, 792, 854. *Principles* § 2, 25, 89, 102-103, 135, 148.
10. *Notebook A*, 542, 769: 'Sensual pleasure is the Summum Bonum. This is the great principle of morality. This once rightly understood, all the doctrines even the severest of the Gospel may be clearly demonstrated.'
11. P. Bayle, *Dictionnaire historique et critique*, articles *Zénon* et *Pyrrhon*, Remarque B: 'Chacun de nous peut bien dire, je sens de la chaleur à la présence du feu; mais non pas *je sais que le feu est tel en lui-méme qu'il me parait*. Voilà quel était le style des anciens pyrrhoniens. Aujourd'hui la nouvelle philosophie tient un langage plus positif: la chaleur, l'odeur, les douleurs etc . . ne sont point dans les objets de nos sens; ce sont des modifications de mon âme; je sais que les corps ne sont point tels qu'ils me paraissent. On aurait bien voulu en excepter l'étendue et le mouvement; mais on n'a pu; car si les objets des sens nous paraissent colorés, chauds, froids, odorans, encore qu'ils ne le soient pas, pourquoi ne pourraient-ils paraître étendus et figurés, en repos et en mouvement, quoiqu'ils n'eussent rien de tel?' P. Bayle renvoie ici, à une objection faite par S. Foucher á Malebranche et observe: 'le père Malebranche n'y répondit pas. Il en sentit bien la force.'
12. *Notebook B*, 185.
13. D.H.P. (I) *Works* II, p. 176: 'the fire effects you only with one simple or uncompounded idea; it follows that this same simple idea is both the intense heat immediately perceived, and the pain.'
14. I. Tipton, *Berkeley, the philosophy of immaterialism*, p. 230-231. See also G.N.A. Vesey, *Berkeley and sensations of heat*, in *The Philosophical Review*, April 1960, 201-210.
15. N.T.V. § 41: 'a mind born blind, beeing made to see, would, at first sight, have no idea of distance by sight (. . .) The objects intromitted by sight would seem to him (. . .) as near as the perception of pain and pleasure or the most inward passions of his soul.'
16. N.T.V. § 59, 147, 159.
17. *Principles* § 1: 'Other collections of ideas constitute a stone, a tree, a book, and the like sensible things; which as they are pleasing or disagreeable, excite the passions of love, hatred, joy, grief and so forth.'
18. *Principles* § 49; *Notebook A*, 886: 'If a man with his eyes shut imagines to himself the sun and firmament you will not say he or his mind is the sun or extended, though neither sun nor firmament be without his mind.'
19. See *supra*, note 1.
20. *Notebook A*, 791.
21. D.H.P. (I), *Works* II, p. 196-197.
22. *Ibidem*, p. 197.
23. D.H.P. (I) *Works* II, p. 197.
24. *Ibidem*, p. 191-192.
25. D.H.P. (I), *Works* II, p. 191.
26. One may observe that a considerable part of *Notebook B* is concerned with a critical examination of Archbishop King's conception of an indifference of desire: see notes 143, 157, 158, 159, 166; 542.
27. Cordemoy, *Le Discernement de l'âme et du corps, Disc. 6*, in *Oeuvres philosophiques*, Paris, 1969, p. 187-188. Cordemoy probably inspired Malebranche in *Recherche de la vérité*, I, ch. XII. IV-V: Explication de trois sortes de sensations de l'âme: erreurs qui accompagnent les sensations. Saint Evremond to Mr. Le Maréchal de Créquy, in *Conversations et autres écrits*

Pleasure and pain versus ideas in Berkeley

philosophiques, édit. A. France, Paris, 1926, p. 187: 'Quelque sagesse dont on se vante en l'âge où je suis, il est mal aisé de connaître si les passions qu'on ne sent plus sont éteintes ou assujetties. Quoi qu'il en soit, dès lors que nos sens ne sont plus touchés des objets et que l'âme n'est plus émue par l'impression qu'ils font sur elle, ce n'est proprement chez nous qu'indolence; mais l'indolence n'est pas sans douceur et songer qu'on ne souffre point de mal est assez à un homme raisonable pour se faire de la joie'. Le concept d'*indolence* est ailleurs explicitement rapporté par Saint Evremond à Epicure.

28. Spinoza, *Ethics*, II, p. XLIII, Scholium.

29. Berkeley, *An essay towards a new theory of vision*, 59, 61, 74, 140.

30. *Works* II, p. 241.

31. *Notebook A*, 852: 'There be two sort of pleasure (. . .) thus the pleasure of eating is of the former sort, of Musick is the later sort. These may be used for recreation, those not but in order to their end.'

32. 'affects', in a broad sense, may include a large group of items (pleasure/unpleasure, emotions, desires). The unity of affects lies only in how damaging they could be to happiness and health for any living creature.

32. Locke, *Essay*, II, XXI, 3: 'Our *idea* therefore of *power*, I think, may well have a place amongst other simple ideas and be considered as one of them, being one of those that make a principal ingredient in our complex ideas of substances, as we shall here after have occasion to observe.'

34. *Principles*, 4, 5, 19-20, 25, 43 (ideas and sensations attending vision), 56 70, 71-72, 74, 78, 81, 87, 90, 99, 136-137, 146, 148-149 — DHP, *Works* II, p. 176, 177, 179-181, 192, 194-195, 203-204, 206, 208, 215, 240-241 (this passage makes clearer than ever that the word sensation is used for any phenomena we are affected with, allowing idea to be the 'objective realtity' of such a phenomenon''. In 'Sensible ideas and sensations' (*Hermathena*, 1967), A.A. Luce takes the contrary way, rather lessening the *idea/sensation* distinction.

35. *Principles*, § 30, 33, 36

36. *Principles*, § 146: 'But if we attentively consider the constant regularity, order or concatenation of natural things, the surprising magnificence, beauty, and perfection of the larger, and the exquisite contrivance of the smaller parts of the creation, together with the exact harmony and correspondence of the whole, but above all the never enough admired laws of pain and pleasure and the instincts or natural inclinations, appetites and passions of animals, I say if we consider all these things (. . .) we shall clearly perceive that they belong to the aforesaid spirit, *who works all in all* and *by whom all things consist*'. See also 65, 151, 153.

37. DHP III, *Works* II, 262: 'There is nothing we either desire or shun, but as it makes, or is apprehended to make some part of our happiness or misery. But what hath happiness or misery, joy or grief, pleasure or pain, to do with absolute existence, or with unknown entities, abstracted from all relation to us? It is evident things regard us only as they are pleasing or displeasing: and they can please or displease only so far forth as they are perceived. Farther therefore we are not concerned.'

Replies

We exegetes know, of course, that Bishop Berkeley attributes as many conceptual infirmities to the doctrine that there are abstract general ideas as he does remedial virtues to the imbibing of tar water. He tells us that the abstraction thesis is one of the chief causes of error in the sciences, and one of the grounds of scepticism, atheism, and irreligion. He finds it also implicated in the arid disputes that take place in philosophy, in particular in logic and metaphysics, disciplines that deal with abstract reasoning. A metaphysical issue *par excellence* is whether houses, mountains, rivers —these are the examples that Berkeley provides of what he calls 'sensible objects'—have an existence distinct from their being perceived. It thus comes as no surprise to the reader of the *Principles* to find Berkeley proposing that those infected with the fantasy that sensible objects exist unperceived could have contracted that disease by exposure to the pernicious humor that there are abstract general ideas.

While acknowledging these general points in his essay, Professor Pappas also wishes to argue that Berkeley has a more specific thesis in mind. He believes that Berkeley holds that there is a strict logical tie between the view that there are abstract general ideas and the *esse* is *percipi* thesis. Though he cites evidence for this position in other works by Berkeley, he basically confines his analysis to the *Principles*. The account he elicits from this work about the logical relationship between the two doctrines commences with the suggestion that the truth of the former is a necessary condition for the falsity of the latter. Finding that this proposal is supported by textual evidence, he moves on to consider whether the relationship can be explicated in terms of sufficient conditions; and finding once again that it can be, he ultimately argues that the tie is one of necessary and sufficient condition, i.e., that the two doctrines, theses, or propositions are logically equivalent. In short, he contends that the two propositions:

1. There are no abstract general ideas, and

2. *Esse* is *percipi*

entail one another. On most standard modal interpretations of such an equivalence relationship, it would follow that it would be impossible for (1) to be false, and for (2) to be true, and conversely. Or if one were to interpret the notion of impossibility in psychological terms, the thesis being advanced would entail that it would be inconceivable (or unimaginable) that (1) could be true and (2) false, and vice-versa. This is a strikingly strong claim, but initially it does not seem inconsistent with the textual evidence, since in his Master Argument in Section 23, and elsewhere, Berkeley does argue that it is impossible to conceive of a sensible object existing unperceived.

Pappas' formulation of the relationship between these two propositions is ingenious and merits his verdict that it is a 'very exciting result' (p.58). So far as I know, his thesis is original. Some writers, to be sure, have come close to suggesting that the first proposition is a necessary condition for the truth of the second, but I cannot think of a commentator who holds that it is both a necessary and sufficient conditon. Even to hold that (1) is a sufficient condition for (2) is a very strong thesis. Thus, we have here an important and arresting exegetical contention, one worth careful assessment. Let us begin by asking whether it does find support within the text.

I cannot find anywhere in the text a single sentence, or a connected set of sentences that expresses this relationship in the progressively precise ways that Pappas construes it. Consider, for example, his so-called Second Argument (p. 58). This he formulates as follows:

1. The *esse* is *percipi* thesis is false only if there are abstract general ideas.

2. There are no abstract general ideas.

3. Therefore, the *esse* is *percipi* thesis is true.

Since no such argument exists verbatim in the *Principles* we are being asked to accept a reconstruction which takes bits and pieces of the text and reorganizes them into the above formal structure. It will be noted that the first premise of the Second Argument does not express an equivalence relationship between the *esse* is *percipi* thesis and the abstract general ideas thesis but only a necessary condition. One of the pieces we might look for in the text is a precise statement to this effect; but none such exists. Nor does the following sentence — proposition No. 7 on p. 52 of Pappas' essay — which does express an equivalence relationship. It says:

> The *esse* is *percipi* thesis is false if and only if there are abstract general ideas.

Once again I cannot find this statement anywhere in the text.

Now Berkeley is famous, or perhaps notorious, for the large amount of explicit argumentation that exists in his works relative to the number of words he employs. This is especially true of the *Principles*. Indeed about half of the 156 sections that make up the *Principles* embody an easily identifiable and formulatable argument. It should therefore give us pause that an argument which Pappas claims to be central to that work is not to be found explicitly formulated anywhere in it. It should give us pause. But to pause is not to invalidate. Pappas' search for a deeper reading of the text seems to me, despite these textual liabilities, to be perfectly justifiable in principle. For it is a familiar fact that what a writer means is not always what he says; and conversely. One indeed recalls certain recent interpretations of Wittgenstein's *Tractatus* which assert that the main thesis of that work is not to be found in the text at all. In any case, it is at least plausible to argue that the meaning of any major philosophical work is not merely to be found in a surface reading of it; that one must go beyond the obvious to elicit a deeper understanding of it. One who seeks such a deeper comprehension is searching for an interpretation of the text, and such interpretations involve doing what Pappas is doing here: i.e., comparing, juxtaposing, breaking up, and reuniting various passages in unexpected ways. The outcome of such a reordering of the text may illuminate it in new and fruitful ways. So granted that the quest for a deeper reading of the *Principles* is justifiable — and indeed I shall propose an alternative interpretation myself at the end of this paper— we should ask: 'How plausible is Pappas' interpretation?' admitting that it stretches the text in certain ways. My answer is that he has bent the text beyond plausibility; and in what now follows I shall try to show why I think so.

There are admittedly several places in the *Principles* where Berkeley alludes to some sort of connection between the two doctrines, but most of these are so exiguous that it would amount to spinning wheels to determine whether they do or do not support Pappas' view. Far and away the most explicit passage that insinuates such a connection is to be found in Section 5. It is this passage that Pappas mostly relies on. It runs as follows:

> 5. 'If we thoroughly examine this tenet it will, perhaps, be found at bottom to depend on the doctrine of abstract ideas. For can there be a nicer strain of abstraction than to distinguish the existence of sensible objects from their being perceived, so as to conceive them existing unperceived.'

This passage clearly shows that Berkeley thinks there is some sort of connection between the view that there are abstract general ideas and that sensible objects exist unperceived. But is it the tight logical connection that Pappas finds? The textual evidence makes this dubious. Note how cautiously Berkeley describes the relationship — Berkeley is not a philosopher generally given to qualification and nuance. He writes:

> 'If we thoroughly examine this tenet it will, *perhaps*, be found at bottom to depend on the doctrine of abstract ideas.'

I emphasize his use of the work 'perhaps' in this quotation. It is hard to see how Berkeley could employ this expression if his view were that there is a tight logical interdigitation between the two doctrines. Moreover, he uses the phrase 'depend on' in explaining the relationship. To say that A depends on B would not normally be taken, in ordinary discourse, to mean that A and B are equivalent in status, but rather that A has some sort of parasitical relationship to B. And even if we translate this location into the idiom of logic it would normally be rendered not as exhibiting an equivalence relationship between A and B but that at most B is a necessary condition for A. For if not B, then not A; but not conversely if A depends on B.

But the main exegetical difficulty here is whether 'depends on' should be glossed as being a logical relationship at all. In his paper Pappas takes 'depends on' to mean 'essential to', which he then interprets as a logical relationship. He is surely on safe ground in thinking that Berkeley is speaking about some kind of dependence relationship but he assumes rather than argues for, let alone proves, that this must be logical in character.

Clearly this is not the only alternative. 'Depends on' can be given plausible non-logical readings, ranging from probalistic to non-evidential relationships entirely. My own view is that Berkeley is speaking about some sort of psychological connection. There are a

142

number of more or less plausible options as to what this might be. Let us render 'depends on' as 'presupposes' where this means something like 'assumes' rather than the kind of logical explication which Strawson gives of that term. One who believes that sensible objects exist unperceived is assuming that he can distinguish in thought between the existence and perception of X. The relationship here described would be between two sets of beliefs, with one of them having a kind of psychological priority. When I, for example, looking at Smith assume that he is British because I hear him speaking English, I am certainly not thinking of his speaking English as a necessary condition of his being British. My assumption can be said to dispose me to believe that he is British; or alternatively we might wish to say that it gives me a good ground or a good reason for believing that Smith is British. One who believes in the possibility of abstracting in this sense will be disposed to believe, or have a good reason for believing, that sensible objects exist unperceived. The relationship as so understood is non-logical.

Of course such alternative possibilities do not show that Pappas' interpretation is wrong, but they give one at least some reason for not accepting it as right. But beyond this, there is a more serious objection to his interpretation. We have seen that if the relationship between the proposition *There are no abstract general ideas* and the proposition *esse* is *percipi* is that of logical equivalence, then it is inconceivable that one of those propositions could be true and the other false. Berkeley, according to Pappas, is arguing that both are true. However, Berkeley's own philosophy gives us good reasons for believing instead that he hold the first proposition to be true and the second false. For he tells us that spirits and God are existing entities and yet in principle are not perceivable. So here we have an instance where a certain x can be conceived as existing unperceived. If Berkeley is right there are no abstract general ideas, and if he is doubly right, then it is possible to conceive of something, say spirits, as existing unperceived. The mere fact that we can imagine the latter possibility entails that the connection between the two doctrines cannot be explicated via necessary and sufficient conditions as Pappas would have it.

Nor will it do to argue that the *esse* is *percipi* principle is not universal in scope but applies only to sensible objects. As Professor Henry Allison has pointed out in his 'Bishop Berkeley's Petitio' this would make Berkeley's argument question begging.

Let me now provide an alternative interpretation of the dependence relationship. Obviously this cannot be defended in the time allotted for this statement so I will simply spell out my own reading of the *Principles*. I think there are two separate lines of argumentation in that work, one of which attempts to show that there are no abstract general ideas and the other of which does not, but is directed instead to proving that *esse* is *percipi*. Let me call the one that does not the 'R' line, because it is a strongly reductive thesis, and the other the 'L' line because in developing it Berkeley is trying to confute Locke. The 'L' line which raises questions about abstraction is mostly submerged in the *Principles*, though we see glimmerings of it just below the surface in the Master Argument of Section 23. Most of the argumentation in the *Principles* consists of a series of variations on the 'R' line. Here is a homogenized version of such an argument:

> The vulgar assume that houses, river, etc. exist when not perceived.
>
> But these are sensible objects.
>
> To say they are sensible objects means that they are perceived by means of the senses.
>
> But what we perceive by the senses are our own sensations, and these are mind-dependent (i.e., exist only when they are being perceived).
>
> Therefore all sensible objects are mind-dependent, and thus the vulgar view entails the contradiction that mind-dependent objects exist when not perceived.

I have spelled this argument out in some detail in order to make it plain that it does not make use of the notion of abstracting or of the product produced by such a process. What it does is to argue that what the vulgar take to be material objects are instead congeries of sensible qualities. It is the reduction of matter to sensation that is being urged here and that is why I call it a reductive argument. Berkeley is claiming that if what the vulgar think of as material objects are congeries of sensible qualities, then it follows they are mind-dependent.

The 'L' line argument is different. It is directed against the Lockean view that it is possible to conceive of matter, described by Locke as a substratum, as distinct from the primary and secondary qualities it supports. This is Locke's version of the famous 'I know not what'. Here the notion of abstracting is fundamental. Locke believes that one can arrive at the concept of existing *per se* by

144

Replies

abstracting. But Berkeley argues that there is no legitimate process of abstraction that will result in such an idea. Sometimes his emphasis is upon the impossibility of the process, sometimes upon the impossibility of the product. The point is that unlike the reductive argument this anti-Lockean move does not try to reduce matter to a heap of sensible qualities. Instead it asserts that those who believe that such a distinction is possible are mistaken.

The two lines of argumentation thus support the thesis of immaterialism in different ways. If these two lines of reasoning were cogent, either would be sufficient to prove immaterialism to be true. But this would show, then, that the doctrine that there are no abstract general ideas cannot be a necessary condition for the truth of the *esse* is *percipi* thesis. The relationship between these lines of argumentation is to be explicated in non-logical terms, as I have argued above. If I am right, Professor Pappas' interpretation, ingenious and interesting as it is, makes too strong a claim.

AVRUM STROLL

Berkeley's denial of the denial of blind agency:
a reply to KENNETH P. WINKLER

Professor Winkler maintains that the denial of blind agency is not explicit in either the *Principles* or the *Dialogues*,[1] not because Berkeley abandoned it, but because he takes it for granted. Given that Berkeley accepts this doctrine elsewhere, it is legitimate to ascribe it to Berkeley in these two works as well. Professor Winkler has documented passages in Descartes, Locke, Malebranche, and Berkeley where each claims that there is no volition without perception — the denial of blind agency thesis. Nevertheless, even though Berkeley may have held this doctrine. at least some of the time, it remains to be established whether Professor Winkler has shown its relevance to Berkeley's discussion of God and the existence of objects.

Two passages quoted by Winkler from the *Principles*, and which are taken by him support the denial of blind agency thesis, seem to me not to do so. The first in Principle 27, Berkeley writes: 'A spirit is one simple, undivided, active being — as it perceives ideas it is called "the understanding", and *as it produces* or otherwise operates upon them it is called "the will".' There is no indication in the

145

portion I have italicized, that Berkeley believes that every act of will presupposes an idea: he obviously holds that there can be idea formation without requiring a precedent identical idea. Principle 28, also quoted by Winkler, makes the same point: 'I find I can excite ideas in my mind at pleasure, and vary and shift the scene as oft as I think fit. *It is no more than willing,* and straightway this or that idea arises in my fancy; and by the same power it is obliterated and makes way for another. This making and unmaking of ideas does very properly denominate the mind active. Thus much is certain and grounded on experience . . .' Again here we see, particularly in the portion which I have italicized, that Berkeley holds that experience reveals cases where willing occurs in the absence of a precedent identical idea. How such willing is possible, I do not pretend to understand, nor do I know of any passages where Berkeley attempts an explanation. In any case, it does seem that Berkeley — at least in the *Principles* — is perfectly comfortable with 'blind agency' willing.

Professor Winkler's employment of the denial of blind agency thesis leads him at one point to write: '. . . divine ideas are not, on my view, superfluous, because without them God would not be unable to perceive, but unable to will.' Now, at one point in the second dialogue, Hylas suggests that although God causes our perceptions, He uses matter as an instrument or occasion: 'by occasion I mean an inactive unthinking being, at the presence whereof God excites ideas in us' (D.163). When Philonous attempts to understand this doctrine he states: 'You acknowledge then God alone to be the cause of our ideas, and that He causes them at the presence of those occasions.' When Hylas agrees, he continues: 'These things which you say are present to God, without doubt He perceives' (D.162). I am not here concerned with Berkeley's objection to the 'material' aspect of such as instrument or occasion (and in the passage I am about to quote, Berkeley also bypasses this concern). I am only concerned with Berkeley's objection to the suggestion that God is unable to make ideas available to us without some instrument or occasion which He perceives. Philonous offers the following criticism:

> Not to insist now on your making sense of this hypothesis, or answering all the puzzling questions and difficulties it is liable to: I only ask whether the order and regularity observable in the series of your ideas, or the course of nature, be not sufficiently accounted for by the wisdom and power of God; and whether it does not derogate

from those attributes to suppose He is *influenced, directed,* or put in mind, when and what He is to act, by an unthinking substance? (D. 163, my italics)

Or again, Philonous says:

> Is it not common to all instruments that they are applied to the doing those things only which cannot be performed by the mere act of our wills . . . We, indeed, who are beings of finite powers, are forced to make use of instruments. And the use of an instrument shows the agent to be limited by rules of another's prescription, and that he cannot obtain his end but in such a way and by such conditions. Whence it seems a clear consequence that the Supreme Unlimited Agent uses no tool or instrument at all. The will of an Omnipotent Spirit is no sooner exerted than executed, *without the application of means,* which, if they are employed by inferior agents, it is not upon account of any real efficacy that is in them, or necessary aptitude to produce any effect, but merely in compliance with the laws of nature or those conditions prescribed to them by the First Cause, *who is Himself above all limitation or prescription whatsoever.* (D.162, my italics)

Berkeley objects to any suggestion that God is 'influenced, directed, or put in mind when and what He is to act'; since God is 'above all limitation or prescription whatsoever', it cannot be true to say that God's will is limited by anything. I submit, therefore, that Berkeley's criticism against Hylas cited above, is equally relevant to Professor Winkler's view. It is true, as Professor Winkler points out, that Berkeley holds that the ideas of all possible worlds are in the divine mind from all eternity: 'All objects are eternally known by God, or, which is the same thing, have an eternal existence in His mind; but when things, before imperceptible to creatures, are, by a decree of God, made perceptible to them, they are said to begin a relative existence with respect to created minds' (D.199). However, divine omnipotence makes it possible for God to will a particular world without, in some sense, needing or using the divine ideas for His act of will.

One last remark on Professor Winkler's position that without the divine ideas God would be unable to will. In both the *Principles* and the *Dialogues,* Berkeley, through Hylas, is usually meticulous in inquiring why an objection which was raised against Hylas' views on matter is not equally effective against Philonous' views on God and ideas. Now Philonous has shown that if God were to require matter as an instrument or occasion, then this would be a limitation on God's omnipotence. It is interesting to note that nowhere is the

147

question raised by Hylas why the need for ideas for the deity's volitions is not equally a limitation on divine omnipotence. On my interpretation this is easily answered: the objection is not raised, and Philonous does not attempt to answer it, because the denial of blind agency is not present in Philonous' argument.

I have already quoted a passage in which Berkeley maintains that all objects are eternally known by God, i.e. have an eternal existence in His mind. Creation for Berkeley involves an act of will by the Deity wherein 'things, before imperceptible to creatures, are. . .made perceptible to them' (D.199). Since God cannot be imposed upon, it follows that the ideas of all objects which are eternally before the divine mind must have been willed by God from all eternity. Now, if Professor Winkler is correct that Berkeley holds the denial of blind agency theory, then in order for all objects (or ideas) to be known by God, He would require ideas or archetypes through which He is able to will that all objects be before His mind. The fact that all objects are eternally known by God does not eliminate the need for these ideas or archetypes, for if the will requires archetypes in order for ideas to be willed, then if ideas are before the divine mind eternally, archetypes must be involved with the divine will eternally. In addition to the fact that this leads to a regress (it is not clear to me whether Professor Winkler recognizes that the regress applies even to the ideas eternally in God's mind), it also leads to the ridiculous position that God requires archetypes even for the ideas He has willed to have eternally in His own mind. Now, if we find this repugant, and then deny that archetypes are involved in the production of the ideas eternally before the deity's mind, then, by a parity of reasoning, there is no need to hold that archetypes are involved in God's willing a particular world. Given the absurdities to which Professor Winkler's solution leads, I suggest that Professor Winkler's solution is not the one which Berkeley should have adopted. And in light of my earlier analysis which showed that Berkeley refuses to allow that God's will is subject to any (necessary) conditions, I am confident that, at least in the *Principles* and the *Three dialogues*, Berkeley did not hold the denial of blind agency thesis.

Berkeley is adamant that all perception, including God's, involves ideas, and (if I am correct in my analysis) he does not agree that all volition, including God's, involves ideas. I should like to offer a suggestion regarding a difference between these claims which might have led Berkeley to accept the first (the perception claim) while rejecting the second (the volition claim).

Replies

It seems to me that the statement 'All perception is the perception of ideas' is analytic; therefore, if we acknowledge that someone (including God) is perceiving something, we must allow that this occurs through ideas. On the other hand, the statement 'All volition involves ideas' is synthetic, and, therefore, if we allow that someone (including God) is willing something, it is still open whether this willing requires certain ideas in the understanding. In particular, if we find the denial of blind agency to be incompatible with God's perfections, then we can grant that God wills something, but deny that certain ideas in the divine mind are necessary for this volition to occur. Perception which does not involve ideas is contradictory and unintelligible; accordingly, for anyone to perceive, ideas must be involved. Volition without ideas is not self-contradictory; and, therefore, the claim that God can will something without ideas is not self-contradictory, and is, in fact, perfectly intelligible. I suggest that the doctrine for which I have argued in the *Principles* and the *Dialogues* would be far more palatable if we dropped the expression 'blind agency' and substituted 'voluntarism'. To say that God acts voluntarily sounds much better than that God wills blindly.

Does Berkeley's account in the *Three dialogues*, of God and His relation to the world, require that he accept a theory of archetypes? An examination of the relevant texts will show that he does not require archetypes for his position.

The first reference to archetypes occurs in the context of the first proof of God's existence. Notice, however, that archetypes are not mentioned in the proof itself:

> To me it is evident, for the reasons you allow of, that sensible things, cannot exist otherwise than in a mind or spirit. Whence I conclude, not that they have no real existence, but that, seeing they depend not on my thought and have an existence distinct from being perceived by me, *there must be some other mind wherein they exist.* As sure, therefore, as the sensible world really exists, so sure is there an infinite omnipresent Spirit, who contains and supports it. (D.153)

This first proof focusses on the involuntary aspect of our ideas of the external world, and on the fact that we must account for the common sense belief that ideas continue to exist even when we are not perceiving them. Archetypes are mentioned in passing when Philonous explains to Hylas (among other things) 'that no idea or archetype of an idea can exist otherwise than in a mind' (D.154). Berkeley, however, gives no indication that the first proof of God's existence involves archetypes — that God cannot will the the world which we perceive without archetypes.

Stanley Tweyman

In the second proof of God's existence, archetypes are included; however, their significance is far from clear:

> It is evident that the things I perceive are my own ideas, and that no idea can exist unless it be in a mind. Nor is it less plain that these ideas or things by me perceived, either themselves or their archetypes, can exist independently of my mind; since I know myself not to be their author. . . They must therefore exist in some other mind, whose will it is they should be exhibited to me. (D. 156)

Although archetypes are mentioned in this passage, it is important to note the following. First, Berkeley appears to be indifferent whether we speak of the ideas perceived and willed by God as ideas or archetypes. And, second, there is nothing in the premises of this second proof of God's existence to countenance the denial of blind agency account of archetypes for which Professor Winkler has argued. Archetypes are mentioned in this proof not as that to which God attends in order to be able to will the perceptions of which I am aware. Rather, archetypes are mentioned as one way of accounting for an object's continued existence and identity. That is, since the things I perceive are my own ideas, and since ideas can only exist when being perceived, whereas things have a continued and independent existence, it follows that either the very ideas I am perceiving are perceived by God, or God has His own ideas (or archetypes) of the objects which finite perceivers apprehend. Since God is always perceiving that which He wills for the perception of finite creatures, the continued existence of objects is explained through the divine perceptions of objects.

At one point in the third dialogue, Hylas raises the following objection:

> . . . the same idea which is in my mind cannot be in yours or in any other mind. Does it not, therefore, follow from your principles that no two can see the same thing? And is this not highly absurd? (D.193)

In a rather lengthy reply, Philonous explains that, according to the 'vulgar acceptation', we do perceive the same thing, whereas if the word 'same' is used in the 'acceptation of philosophers', then it may or may not be possible for different people to perceive the same things, depending upon the particular definition employed. In other words, the dispute about sameness or difference in this case is verbal: '. . .who sees not that all the dispute is about a word, to wit, whether what is perceived by different persons may yet have the

term "same", applied to it?' (D.194). Philonous concludes by point-
ing out that materialists have no advantage in regard to this topic:

> Are you not yet satisfied men may dispute about identity and
> diversity without any real difference in their thoughts and opinions
> abstracted from names? Take this further reflection with you — that
> whether matter be allowed to exist or no, the case is exactly the same
> as to the point in hand. For the materialists themselves acknowledge
> what we immediately perceive by our senses to be our own ideas.
> Your difficulty, therefore, that no two see the same thing makes
> equally against the materialists and me. (D.135)

To Hylas' suggestion that materialists have an advantage over
Philonous because 'they suppose an external archetype to which
referring their several ideas they may truly be said to perceive the
same thing', Philonous replies:

> And (not to mention your having discarded those archetypes) so
> may you suppose an external archetype on my principles; *external*, I
> mean to your own mind, though, indeed, it must be supposed to
> exist in the mind which comprehends all things; but then, this serves
> all the ends of *identity*, as well as if it existed out of a mind. (D.195)

One of the interesting features of this passage is that Berkeley is not
keen to include archetypes in his position: this, I submit, would be
extremely odd if Professor Winkler's account of the denial of blind
agency is Berkeley's position, whereas, on my reading of Berkeley,
this is not at all odd since God does not require ideas or archetypes
before His will can be exercised. A second interesting feature, it
seems to me, is that Berkeley says that on his principles we may
suppose an external archetype: again, this would be extremely odd
on Professor Winkler's reading of Berkeley, but not odd on mine.
Hylas' position is that materialists can account for an object's
identity through the continued existence of the physical object. The
physical object serves as an archetype in virtue of its abiding
character amidst the variability of our perceptions. Berkeley's position is that because God is always perceiving what we perceive at
various times, God's perception can serve as the archetype in virtue
of its abiding character amidst the variability of our perceptions.
The important point to note, however, is that Berkeley is not
concerned with archetypes because he is not concerned with the
topic of the identity of objects. On Professor Winkler's account,

Stanley Tweyman

Berkeley *should be* concerned with archetypes because, without them, the divine will could not be exercised.

STANLEY TWEYMAN

Notes

1. All references to Berkeley's *Principles* and *Dialogues* are taken from George Berkeley, *Principles, dialogues and correspondence*, edited by Colin M. Turbayne, The Library of Liberal Arts, published by Bobbs-Merrill Company, Inc., Indianapolis, New York, Kansas City, 1965.

Money, wealth, and Berkeley's doctrine of signs: a reply to PATRICK KELLY

At the center of Kelly's paper is this train of thought. Before he came to grips with Ireland's special economic situation, Berkeley held quite conventional views, where he held any; after taking full cognizance of Irish conditions, Berkeley reached the judgment that the Mercantilist foreign trade agenda spelled disaster for Ireland. On the basis of that judgment Berkeley arrived at a distinctive theory of *wealth*, from which he derived his theory of *money* as a ticket or counter. My response centers on a critical evaluation of this claim, but first I will mention several other highlights in Kelly's remarks.

Kelly makes us question how *consistent* Berkeley was about paper-money since he wanted to back paper bills with land. Was Schumpeter right? Was Berkeley a concealed metallist? Then come questions concerning the *originality* of Berkeley's theory of money. For Locke held that in an isolated economy — and for Kelly, Berkeley's program was to isolate the Irish economy — the material used for money was arbitrary. Finally, Kelly revises the received opinion of Berkeley as an anti-Mercantilist. For him, Berkeley is less interested in condemning Mercantilism than in distinguishing rich and poor countries. Kelly adds that, like the Mercantilists, Berkeley favored strong state guidance of the economy.

Turning to Kelly's central thesis that it was Berkeley's rejection of Mercantilism for Ireland which led to his distinctive theory of wealth, and in turn, to his views on money, I will, *first*, sketch an

Replies

alternative view which locates the logic of Berkeley's conceptions of wealth and money in the basic themes and principles of his philosophy, above all in his critical doctrine of signs. *Second,* I will raise some difficulties in Kelly's case for his thesis. *Third,* I will question whether Berkeley was the opponent of foreign trade for poor countries that Kelly makes him out to be.

When Kelly refers to Berkeley's American experience as 'the one respect in which he differed so notably from contemporary Irish writers', he omits an obvious further difference. George Berkeley was an original and important philosopher. I believe that his distinctive theories of wealth and money return us to the pervasive principles and themes of his philosophy. Though Kelly makes several observations in this vein, they remain undeveloped. Kelly notes Petty's distinction between 'local' and 'universal' wealth, the latter being money in the form of silver and gold. Later Kelly observes: 'The "universal" wealth that gold and silver constituted for Petty and Locke is for Berkeley a general idea without a corresponding reality.' Kelly returns to this at the close of his paper, stating that Berkeley 'reversed the distinction drawn by Petty . . . and demonstrated that "local" wealth was indeed real and "universal".' I want to pursue Kelly's leads and claim that the distinctiveness of Berkeley's thinking on wealth and money comes not from Irish conditions but from his critical doctrine of signs: for Berkeley, money is a sign of wealth.

Berkeley's rejection of the Petty-Locke theory of 'universal' wealth has the same logic as his rejection of Locke's abstract ideas. Both are rooted in Berkeley's theory of *general* signs. A fanciful form of reasoning concerning signs, a 'semiotic fallacy' that Berkeley repeatedly uncovered is the positing of an abstraction as the unique referent of a general sign, be it a *word,* a *number,* or *money.* For Berkeley, no one, unique thing corresponds to a general sign. To identify money with 'universal' wealth is really to commit a double fallacy, the first: to think that there is any abstract entity such as 'universal' wealth, the second: to collapse the sign into the thing signified or purportedly signified. Thus money, the sign, is identified with what, according to the first 'semiotic fallacy', it supposedly signifies, namely 'universal' wealth. Now Berkeley was no more opposed to money than to general words or numbers, but general signs must be properly understood. They refer not to any one, unique, abstract idea or thing, rather they are general by referring indifferently to any one of a group of particulars. Hence money refers indifferently to power or property *in the particular.*

Patrick Murray

Kelly observes that Berkeley's two most renowned economic doctrines are: (1) money is not universal wealth incarnate and (2) money need not be silver or gold. I have just considered the first, now I turn to the second, again placing Berkeley's economic innovation in the context of his doctrine of signs. In the *Essay towards a new theory of vision* Berkeley employs his doctrine of signs to show that visible and tangible ideas are completely distinct (as are money and wealth); that there is no necessary connection between the two (as the material of money is arbitrary); and that there is no common object, no abstract matter, to which they can be referred (as there is no 'intrinsic value' common to money and wealth). Berkeley's answer to the Molyneux problem is startling, for we presume a necessary connection between the visible and the tangible. People in Berkeley's day likewise were ready to assume that there is nothing arbitrary about silver and gold as representatives of wealth. What makes the 'semiotic fallacies' with respect to 'visual language' so intractable is relevant to the difficulty in rooting out this 'prejudice' which identifies money with silver and gold. It is the *constancy* and *universality* of the 'visual language' which make the fallacies concerning it more ingrained than those associated with humanly instituted languages. Berkeley hypothesized that if there were only one universal and invariable language spoken from birth 'it would be the opinion of many that the ideas of other men's minds were properly perceived by the ear, or had at least a necessary and inseparable tie with the sounds that were affixed to them'.[1] Silver and gold were close to being a universal language of wealth; it is not surprising that such universal and constant conjunction should have been mistaken for necessary connection in this case as well.

The burden of my case against Kelly's main thesis lies in the alternative I just outlined, but there are other considerations. *First*, how can Kelly grant that Berkeley's essay of 1721 contains ideas about wealth found in the *Querist* when he is arguing that Berkeley's theory of wealth came from his later rejection of foreign trade? The suggestion that Berkeley's *Querist* is a turnabout from his position in the early *Essay*, one made in response to his closer acquaintance with Irish conditions seems wrong to me. Several years *before* that essay Berkeley had written in *Guardian* 77: 'Words and money are both to be regarded as only marks of things. And as the knowledge of the one, so the possession of the other is of no use, unless directed to a further end.'[2] *Second*, Kelly's decisive move is not any of the ones *within* his 14-step reconstruction of the *Querist's* argument but the prior inference from Berkeley's rejection of foreign trade to the

154

view of wealth described in the first proposition. How is *this* inference made? What is compelling about it? Why didn't Petty make it, as he endorsed the same view on Irish trade? Moreover, Berkeley's Query 548 stands Kelly's thesis on its head: 'Whether the benefits of a domestic commerce are sufficiently understood and attended to; and whether the cause thereof be not the prejudiced and narrow way of thinking about gold and silver?'[3] Here the case for *domestic* trade is based on Berkeley's view of money.

Now I briefly consider Kelly's point that Berkeley's stress on Ireland's domestic economy was not so much a rejection of Mercantilism as it was a theory of development for poor countries. *First,* Berkeley rejected for *any* country, rich or poor, the Mercantilist rationale for foreign trade, namely, to stock up silver and gold. *Second,* Berkeley cited Switzerland as a case of a rich country with little foreign trade.[4] *Third,* Berkeley was by no means unequivocally opposed to foreign trade for Ireland: in fact, he offered a list of suggestions for export goods including lace, hemp, and flax. *Fourth,* Berkeley's chief reasons against foreign trade in Ireland's case were not generic to economies of poor countries. Ireland's trade was heavily restricted by the English out of the jealousy of trade sentiments Kelly mentioned. Berkeley opposed such restrictions but thought that Ireland could prosper even under these adverse conditions, which were worsened by the absentee problem. The Irish found themselves exporting provisions, which Berkeley thought would be better consumed at home. It is not clear, though, that Berkeley opposed exporting goods for which there was not a pressing domestic need. Query 174 begins, 'Whether it would not be wise so to order our trade as to export manufactures rather than provisions?'[5] On the *import* side, it is again the *content* of the trade, not its *level* to which Berkeley objects. Query 554 asks: 'Whether foreign imports that tend to promote industry should not be encouraged, and such as have a tendency to promote luxury should not be discouraged?'[6]

In closing, I will comment on the extent to which Berkeley was an anti-Mercantilist. Berkeley certainly rejected the Mercantilist hoarding of silver and gold, but he went on to question the project of blindly accumulating riches of any sort. Just as he criticized the *scientism* of those 'grammarians of nature' who thought that natural science was the sole interpreter of the book of nature, Berkeley criticized the *economism* of those writers who shortened their view to the 'grammar' of commerce and neglected its broader purposes. For Berkeley, the Mercantilists were guilty of bad 'grammar' and

Patrick Murray

economism. This is relevant to Kelly's observation that Berkeley agreed with Mercantilism in opposing economic liberalism and giving strong powers to the state. Whereas the Mercantilists relied on state power for economic ends, Berkeley's case for state involvement mixed technical economic considerations with moral, religious, educational, and aesthetic concerns. While the Mercantilist state was a powerful force in the creation of '*homo economicus*', Berkeley was set against cutting the economy loose from its religious and moral moorings.

PATRICK MURRAY

Notes

1. George Berkeley, *An essay towards a new theory of vision*, No. 66, in *The works of George Berkeley*, I (London, 1948), pp. 195-196.
2. George Berkeley, '*Guardian* Essay VII', (No. 77. Tuesday, June 9), in *The works of George Berkeley*, VII (London, 1955), p. 212.
3. George Berkeley, *The querist*, Qu. 548, in *The works of George Berkeley*,VI (London, 1953), p. 150.
4. *Querist*, Qu. 420-423, p. 139.
5. *Querist*, Qu. 174, p. 119.
6. *Querist*, Qu. 554, p. 151.

The entries in Berkeley's Notebooks:
a reply to BERTIL BELFRAGE

I agree with much of what Dr Belfrage says in this paper. There seems, as he suggests, to have been an early phase in which Berkeley held that a word is being used intelligibly only if there is an idea corresponding to it. This was Berkeley's view in 'Of infinites' and in entry 696 of *Notebook A* as that entry was first written down by Berkeley:

> . . . Let him (my Reader) not regard my Words any otherwise than as occasions of bringing into his mind determin'd ideas so far as they fail of this they are Gibberish, Jargon & deserve not the name of Language. . .

This was also Berkeley's view in entries 354 and 356 in Notebook B, both of which Berkeley labelled as axioms. Berkeley deployed this account of what it is for a word to have meaning as part of his

156

attack on mathematicians who thought that we can reason about infinitesimals. Belfrage points out that towards the end of Notebook A a different position is presented. Berkeley now has a place for signs which do not have ideas associated with them. There are, as entry 768 puts it, 'sciences purely verbal' and these include arithmetic and algebra. The new position allows that a word may have significance even if there is no idea answering to it.

Perhaps it is the case that we can infer from these remarks in the manuscript Introduction, or draft Introduction, to the *Principles*, that theological considerations played some part in this shift, for Berkeley writes there that

> [we] are told that the good things which God hath prepared for them that love him are such as eye hath not seen nor ear heard nor hath it enter'd into the heart of man to conceive. What man will pretend to say these words of the inspir'd writer are empty and insignificant? And yet who is there that can say they bring into his mind clear and determinate ideas of the good things in store for them that love God?[1]

He seems here to acknowledge that some religious discourse is meaningful in spite of the fact that no ideas correspond to it. And I agree that in the draft of the Introduction and in the first sermon he makes clear that language can have emotive meaning and that this is the sort of meaning that some religious discourse has.[2]

It seems plain that Berkeley, as an Anglican cleric, ought not to have been satisfied with ensuring only a non-cognitive meaning for religious discourse. Surely he thought that propositions which express orthodox Christian views about God, the afterlife, and so on, describe how things are. Neither the account of emotive meaning which he relies upon in an attempt to explain how such propositions have meaning, nor the account of instrumental meaning which he relies upon in his discussion of 'sciences purely verbal' but which he does not introduce when discussing religious discourse, would explain how the propositions of orthodox Christianity can describe how things are. So if the introduction of either of these accounts of how language may sometimes be meaningful, were intended by Berkeley as a response to theological objections which William King or Peter Browne or other members of the audience raised when Berkeley read 'Of Infinites' to the Dublin Philosophical Society on 19 November, 1707, as Belfrage suggests, Berkeley would deserve low marks for this response.[3] It would seem, at any rate, that Berkeley had not thought the matter out with care.

Robert McKim

I suggest, however, that what Dr Belfrage refers to, in his title and throughout his paper, as a *clash* might better be referred to as a *change* or *shift* or *transition* or *development*. Certainly there is what might be referred to as a 'clash' between the earlier belief that words are meaningful only if they refer to ideas, and the later belief that words are sometimes meaningful even if they do not refer to ideas. There is, to be sure, no harm in referring to Berkeley's transition from the earlier view to the latter view — or, if *this* is what is meant, to the relationship between the earlier and the later view — as a 'clash', provided that we bear in mind that what is being described is a *change* of view.

And there are many such changes to be observed in the *Notebooks*. If we accept the standard ordering of the entries — that is, if we accept that Berkeley wrote the entries in the order in which they are to be found in Add. Ms. 39305 in the British Library and in the standard editions — then we find important changes in his view of the mind and of how extension is to be shown not to be external to the mind, for example, although he seems to have been an immaterialist from the outset.

So why does Belfrage think that the shift which he discusses is important? He hints at his reasons only in the first and last paragraphs of his paper. In the former he tells us that in this paper he is taking 'a first constructive step towards an alternative reading of the Notebooks'; and in the latter he tells us that in this paper 'the *first* piece of evidence in . . . a broader project' is contributed. The broader project is to challenge the 'reversed-order theory', the orthodox view according to which Berkeley wrote Notebook B before Notebook A, and according to which Berkeley reached his mature standpoint at the beginning of Notebook A.

Now Belfrage shows that there is a very important respect in which what is to be found at the beginning of Notebook A is *not* so mature. And he points out that the view of the mind that is expressed in entry 580 of Notebook A also seems to be immature:

> Mind is a congeries of Perceptions. Take away Perceptions & you take away the Mind put Perceptions and you put the mind.

So far so good. However, this is very weak evidence against the reversed-order theory; in fact, it is not evidence against it at all. For the reversed-order theory is compatible with the view that *some* of Berkeley's views were still at a fairly early stage of development when he began Notebook A. We would have evidence against the

158

reversed-order theory only if, for example, the mature position at the end of A were also to be found in Notebook B. But Belfrage does not provide such evidence. And even *that* evidence would be far from decisive since Berkeley might have at one time accepted some view, later rejected it, and yet later returned to it. A convincing case could be made only by considering many central aspects of Berkeley's development. In any case there is nothing in Dr Belfrage's analysis of the shift in Berkeley's view of whether or not terms must signify ideas if they are to be meaningful, which suggests that the entries in the notebooks were not written more or less in the order in which they are now to be found. In short, we do not have, here, 'the first piece of evidence . . . in a broader project'.

A part of Belfrage's view of the relevance of the fact that there is such a shift or change in the notebooks for the broader project seems to be this. If there are two blocks of entries in A, one before the shift and one after it, then *perhaps* B, or part of B, was written after the writing of the first block and before the writing of the second block. This is certainly *possible*, but that it is actually the case would need to be established on other grounds.

The broader project is an interesting one, but it remains to be seen whether or not it can be carried out. The commentators certainly have assumed that the entries in the Notebooks were written in the order in which they are to be found, with the entries in Notebook B being written before those in Notebook A. It has, therefore, been assumed that we can follow at least part of the course of Berkeley's philosophical development by examining the entries in the notebooks in the order in which they are to be found. So Dr Belfrage's broader project, if successfully executed, would have important implications for our understanding of Berkeley's development. His approach might also lead to new insights into Berkeley's views in his major writings, although this is something that would need to be examined.

However, there are some reasons why I am doubtful that his view can be adequately defended; I am doubtful, in other words, that the broader project *can* be executed successfully. I think that the traditional view that the entries in B were written first and those in A last, and that the entries were written in the order in which we find them is *more or less* correct. In order to *show* this I would need to examine all of the arguments which Dr Belfrage has offered elsewhere for his suggestions about the order in which the entries were written and some other pieces of evidence, and this is impossible here. I will, however, make a few brief observations.

First, entries which concern how it is best to present his views, what phrases to use, and so on, are much more common in A than they are in B. This suggests that in A Berkeley has decided on what he wants to say and is now deciding how to present it.

Second, I think that A.A. Luce's observations about the occurrences of the term 'idea' have something to them, in spite of the objections of Professor Furlong and others. Luce noticed that, as the entries have traditionally been ordered, in the early entries Berkeley wrote the word 'idea' with a lower case 'i', in the late entries he wrote it with a capital 'I', and in between he wrote it with both. It has been objected that there are manuscripts written after the putative latest entries in the notebooks, in which the word 'idea' is written with a lower case 'i',and that therefore we ought not to attempt to base any claims about the order of the writing of the entries on the orthography of the word 'idea' in the notebooks. But the change which Luce observed is so evident in the notebooks that one is inclined to say that its importance is not undermined by the fact that Berkeley later reverts to the use of the lower case 'i' when writing 'idea'.

Third, and most important, there seems to be a development in doctrine throughout the notebooks, taking them in the order in which we find them. This can not be shown in any detail here, but I will consider one important example. The belief that the existence of all things other than spirits consists in being perceived seems to be a belief which Berkeley hit on in the course of writing Notebook B, and a belief which he takes for granted throughout *all* of Notebook A. I think it is not clear where precisely in the course of Berkeley's writing of the entries in Notebook B he first presented this belief. Part of the reason for this is that there are early entries in which Berkeley took positions which resemble, or are suggestive of, the belief that for things other than spirits, to be is to be perceived. It probably is the case that the first allusion to the new belief is to be found at entry 279/80 in Notebook B:

> I wonder not at my sagacity in discovering the obvious tho' Amazing truth, I rather wonder at my stupid inadvertency in not finding it out before, 'tis no Witchcraft to see . . . . Our simple ideas are so many simple thoughts or perceptions, & that a perception . . . . cannot exist without a thing to perceive it or any longer than it is perceiv'd . . . .

It seems clear that in entry 437 of Notebook A the new belief is being accepted:

Replies

Impossible anything Besides that wch thinks & is thought on should exist.

At the end of B and at the beginning of A the new belief seems to be what Berkeley has in mind when he refers to 'the principle', or sometimes 'my principle(s)', 'this principle' or 'my doctrine'. (See e.g. PC 285, 291, 304, 305, 407, 410, 411, 474, 474a, 589.) And throughout A he seems to be exploring the implications of his new belief, as well as considering how to present it (see e.g. 424, 427, 427a, 429, 472, 491, 517, 517a, 528, 550, 563, 588, 633, 863). I am aware that this one case does not *prove* that the traditional view, which Belfrage opposes, is correct, but it is, at any rate, the sort of evidence which seems to constitute a difficulty for his broader project.

To conclude, I agree with Dr Belfrage's observations about an important change in Berkeley's in the course of Notebook A. However, I am not convinced, indeed I deny, that this change has the significance which Dr. Belfrage believes it to have.

ROBERT MCKIM

Notes

1. See *Works of Berkeley*, edited by Luce & Jessop, Vol, 2, p. 137.
2. See *Works*, Vol. 2, pp. 137-140 and *Works*, Vol. 7, pp. 10-14.
3. David Berman, in 'Berkeley's semantic revolution: 19 November 1707-January 1708' (forthcoming in *History of European ideas*, 1986), makes similar suggestions about Berkeley's reasons for changing his mind. At the end of his paper Berman quotes from a letter dated 27 March 1710, in which King indicates some displeasure at Berkeley's ordination. Could it be that even if Berkeley had attempted to respond to King's objections, King thought the response to be none too impressive?

D. M. Armstrong

The heart of Berkeley's metaphysics?
a reply to ERNEST SOSA

Ernest Sosa has certainly given us something to think about with his paper 'Berkeley's master stroke'. It is an interesting, and I think quite novel, hypothesis that in Berkeley's philosophy there is no fundamental nexus or copula except perceiving (with conceiving taken to be a sub-species of perceiving) and willing. In giving his paper at Dublin, Sosa brought perceiving, conceiving and willing under the single umbrella term 'minding'. There is no fundamental nexus or copula except minding.

As Sosa points out, Berkeley has a clear motive for resisting *attribution* as a fundamental nexus. For if it *is* admitted, then the case against material substance, thing-having-properties, is weakened, perhaps fatally. This is a quite new point to me.۱

But in the end, Sosa is inclined to think, Berkeley is forced to re-admit attribution.

First, Sosa objects, 'Being an idea would seem to be exemplified by each idea, being a quality by each quality, being a spirit by each spirit'. All Sosa can suggest on Berkeley's behalf here is a 'radical Nominalism'.

Perhaps Sosa is selling Berkeley a little short here. A Resemblance Nominalism might be attempted. The particulars involved would have an especially low degree of resemblance to each other, but, it could be maintained, this resemblance of low degree is an objective one. Perhaps Sosa would think that this move treats *resemblance* as a fundamental nexus additional to minding. But I am not sure that this consequence follows. Resemblance is an internal relation, logically supervenient upon the nature of the resembling things. It is plausible to take this to have the consequence that the resemblance is *exhausted* by the natures of the resembling things. But if so, resemblance can hardly be a fundamental nexus. Hence, if Berkeley can treat the natures involved as purely particular, but objectively resembling, entities, then perhaps he need not embrace radical Nominalism.

Sosa canvasses a second objection. He says 'ideas may include constituent qualities', and asks 'is not complexity then exemplified by such ideas?'. This would be attribution again.

One might reply on Berkeley's behalf that the notion of complexity need involve no more than the notion of a plurality of parts, that parts are not properties, and that even *the having of parts* is not a real property either. But whether or not this is true, Sosa has uncovered

162

Replies

a fundamental difficulty for (Sosa's) Berkeley. For complexity normally involves not merely a plurality of parts — a mere aggregate of parts — but the *relation* of these parts. And *relation* would be an addition to the allegedly single nexus of *minding*.

As Sosa indicates, some relations Berkeley can deal with. For instance, *to the left of* can be analyzed in terms of *is perceived to be to the left of*, which is just a particular case of perceiving, and so a case of minding. But, Sosa points out further, what of the fact that, by the arrangement of God, 'various spirits have various ideas in various ways'. *That* complexity involves spirits and ideas standing in relations which cannot be analyzed in terms of the nexus of *minding*.

Sosa does not see how a (Sosa) Berkeley is to solve the problem. Neither do I. It is not much use to trade in properties if you have to take on relations. It is true that the thing-property nexus is avoided here. But once relations are admitted, Berkeley will lack an argument against the conception that physical objects are bundles of qualities, but where the bundling relation is *not* constituted by being perceived.

So, even on Sosa's own showing, Sosa's Berkeley has problems. But, as I will now argue, the problem for Berkeley is even worse. At the centre of Berkeley's metaphysics lies a dilemma. Are ideas modes (attributes) of spirits? Berkeley flirted with this at one time ('manners of the existence of persons', *Notebooks*, 24). Sosa has perhaps shown us why Berkeley could not go that way. He could not allow attribution. Are ideas 'in' the mind as parts? As we know, Berkeley flirted with that one too. But to make the relation of ideas to minds into the relation of part to whole leads to the horrors of Hume's bundle theory. Sosa would once again point out that the relations which are required to tie the bundle together cannot be analyzed in terms of perceiving and willing (though Hume had a sporting shot at it).

Ideas are not attributes of the mind, nor are they parts. As a result, ideas must be thrust outside the mind. They are perceived by the mind, and unable to exist outside the perceptual relation, but they are distinct from the mind. And this, I suggest, strikes a fatal blow at the *dialectics* of Berkeley's position. For how then is the *esse est percipi* to be demonstrated?

It was supposed to be done by arguing that cherries, gloves and so forth are nothing but sensations, which are mental. But if they are later asserted to be distinct from the mind, then an argument will be needed to say that they cannot exist independently of

D. M. Armstrong

perception ('unsensed sensibilia'), and, still worse, that matter cannot so exist.

The fact is, I believe, that various of Berkeley's fundamental principles — perhaps we should say intellectual drives — cannot be brought into coherence. His greatness does not lie in the high degree of internal organization of his metaphysical system. Perhaps, as Sosa has so interestingly suggested, there is a drive in his thought to a single copula — the 'minding' nexus. But I doubt that this drive can be seen as a single master-stroke, underlying the whole of his system.

D. M. ARMSTRONG

*This paper is a reply to Professor Ernest Sosa's paper 'Berkeley's master stroke', published in *Essays on Berkeley*, ed. J. Foster and H. Robinson (Clarendon Press: Oxford University Press, 1985), 59-81.

164

Index of Names

Index of Names

Index of Names

Index of Names

Index of Subjects

Index of Subjects

Index of Subjects